Get the kayak

Learn to fish by kayak:

the most overlooked, effective, efficient, and convenient way to catch more fish, fish more often, fish with less hassle, and save money doing it !

From small remote ponds to rivers or oceans:

Fish with incredible stealth in inaccessible areas !

Learn from the experts in fresh and saltwater:

Get expert advice from experienced professional and expert kayak anglers from US, Canada, & Mexico

Get advice on buying, choosing, customizing, and rigging kayaks for fishing

Get home customizing techniques for installing live bait tanks, rodholders, depthfinders, building homemade kayak carts and much more

Get help with how to customize an old kayak

Get special chapters on expert techniques for kayak flyfishing, lure fishing, live bait fishing, big fish fighting and handling

Get email contacts of experienced kayakfishermen who are anxious to help you get started

Get lists of kayakfishing guides

Get lists of kayakfishing friendly paddleshops

Get lists of internet website addresses for kayaks, kayakfishing advice, accessories, guides, instructors, lessons, bulletin boards, maps and information on new cutting edge products

This book was written to educate, entertain, and to present the activities and techniques of individuals engaged in the sport. The information presented in this book does not warrant the safety of the activities or techniques presented. Weather, wild creatures, and outdoor environments are all unpredictable. The author and Coelacanth Communications shall have neither liability nor responsibility to any person or entity with respect to any loss or damage caused, or alleged to be caused, directly or indirectly by the information contained in this book.

KAYAKFISHING:

The Revolution

by Ken Daubert

First Edition

Coelacanth Communications

ISBN 0-9678098-2-7

Library of Congress #2001116094

KAYAKFISHING:

The Revolution

by Ken Daubert

Published by:

Coelacanth Communications
3323 S.E. 2nd Street
Ocala, FL 34471

First edition

Printed in the United States of America

Acknowledgements

With great thanks, I would like to acknowlede all of the members of the kayakfishing and kayaking community who gave aid in the writing of this book. Many of them are mentioned and featured in this book. I would especially like to thank those who wrote copy material, shared their stories and photos in order to make this book possible. There can be no other sport where the participants are more friendly and enthusiastic to share information. I would, in particular, like to thank my daughter Danielle for all of her efforts at photography on my behalf.

Photo credits

Page 21- Jeff Krieger, page 22- Wade Clark, page 38 - Ken Sigvardson, page 46 - Gary Bulla, page 48 - Ken Sigvardson, page 50 - Jeff Krieger, page 51 - Colin Harrison, page 57 - Ken Sigvardson, page 77 - Jackson Reade, page 79 - Mark Ambrozic, page 87 - Jackson Reade, page 102 - Ocean Kayak, page 102 - Jeff Krieger, page 115 - Ocean Kayak, page 118 - Roleez Wheel Systems, page 142 - Tribalance Kayaks, page 210 - George Whillock, page 220 - Jeff Krieger, page 223 - Mark Ambrozic, page 225 - Gary Bulla, page 229 - Ken Sigvardson

All other photographs are credited to Danielle Daubert and illustrations to Ken Daubert.

About The Author

Ken Daubert began sneaking away from the house to the *Minneyhole* and *The Pond*, nearly worrying his poor Mother to death, at the tender age of four. From there, he kept going on a rusty old bicycle twenty six miles roundtrip through the south Jersey countryside, pumping the pedals up many a steep hill and past numerous long since dead, but remembered, grouchy dogs along the way to his favorite farm pond. He kept going. He fished freshwater and saltwater from oceans to mountain streams with flyrods and conventional tackle throughout the United States, Canada and Europe. Along the way, he served in the Army and the Navy, and earned a degree in Biology and Environmental Sciences. He became a published author in major outdoor fishing magazines. He became a nationally recognized taxidermist with a client list that reads like a Who's Who List in the outdoor and sports world. Headquartering on Half Moon Lake in the Ocala National Forest in central Florida, he became a U.S. Coast Guard liscensed captain and fishing guide for 19 years. He was featured in almost every major outdoor fishing magazine as a top taxidermist and fishing guide for trophy largemouth bass, saltwater flats and flyfishing. He has been a lifetime designer of fishing lures and flies, and many of his fishing lure and fly designs have been featured in the outdoor magazines. He built a 14,000 gallon outdoor aquarium in his backyard to do aquatic photography and to study fish behavior. Along with several partners, he designed, promoted and marketed the famous Banjo Minnow fishing lure which became the hottest selling fishing lure in the country. He served as vice president of Banjo Buddies Inc. and was one of the producers of the infomercial that was nominated for four international awards and actually won two of the four categories. He appeared in the original infomercial and made appearances on QVC. Ken also did much of the underwater photography for Bill Dance's infomercial *Soundbite* and has been a member of several other corporations as a consultant to manufacture and promote fishing lures and products. He's still going, but mostly by kayak.

Preface

I had been searching for something ever since I began fishing at about four years old. I started out on the bank casting from shore at any available opening in the shoreline shrubbery. Eventually, I stepped into the water and began my wading career wherever the bottom was not too treacherous. I experimented with Huck Finn style makeshift rafts in order to expand my fishable range. Later, I even tried an inflatable raft. My fishing improved greatly with jonboats rigged with trolling motors, and tubefloats were great where you couldn't get a boat or trolling motor battery close enough to the lake to launch. Canoes worked great sometimes when the wind did not blow me around. Bigger, fancier, more expensive rigs brought a new freedom of distance, luxury, convenience, and even effectiveness. They also brought new hassles of monthly payments, insurance, maintenance, repairs, trailers, electronics and corrosion. Still, I pressed on in my search for the ultimate fishing craft until my ultimate fishing machine had six twelve volt batteries, three trolling motors, two livewells, raised platforms fore and aft, and two or three guide clients to pay for it all. All the time, my subconcious was wrestling with the idea that somewhere, somehow there was a better, simpler way. Then I found it. It had the portability of a tubefloat and even better distance and windward paddling characteristics than a canoe. It revolutionized my fishing and opened up a new world of angling adventure. So, I am here to tell you about it.

Table of Contents

Chapter One

Join The Revolution

Author with Gulf of Mexico tarpon

The purpose of this book is to convince you to join the revolution to combine two of our greatest and most popular outdoor recreation and nature oriented sports into one exciting and enjoyable venture, and to help you get past any initial hassles or frustrations in your early attempts to catch sportfish from a kayak. This book is not meant to be the authority or last word on the subject. This book is written for the benefit of those fishermen who have not thought of or tried fishing from a kayak, kayakers who have not yet tried fishing from their kayak, and those who have neither fished nor kayaked but think that it might be something they would like to try. Further, this book is intended to promote and popularize this sport that seems to be just at its beginning. Outdoor writers have just begun to write articles about this sport, and at the time of this writing, there were no other books on this subject.

Stream smallmouth

However, this frontier sport does have early pioneers and heroes. Some have been more or less quietly kayakfishing for a long time without much interaction or communication with kindred spirits: Simply because it was a good idea, enjoyable and effective. Some have performed heroic feats, paddling far to the horizon and battling with outsized fish in such a manner as to rival Hemmingway's *The Old Man and The Sea*. Some are busy working out the new ideas that will become the very nature, classic content and methods of our sport. Others are busy designing and inventing all manner of kayak accessories to make our efforts more enjoyable, efficient and effective. Teachers, guides and outfitters are emerging to give lessons and take the uninitiated out for a day of safe, educational and valuable initial experience. Due to the Internet, it is an evolution at an ever increasing rate. Increased communication through websites, community bulletin boards, and email are transferring ideas between experienced and new kayakfishermen at a pace that would not be possible in *less-connected* times.

Flyrodding for bass

To all new kayakfishermen, whether you are a fisherman who has never tried a kayak, or a kayaker who has never seriously tried fishing from his kayak, or one of those folks who has neither fished nor kayaked, your fellow kayakfishermen would like to extend an enthusiastic welcome.

To the fishermen, your fishing knowledge is a great headstart. Kayaking is relatively easy compared to understanding the subtleties of catching fish. You already know the fish, places and techniques. You will quickly learn to apply the advantages of a kayak to your fishing. Get started as soon as possible. Don't put it off or you will regret not having started sooner. But first read this book. It could save you some mistakes and get you started on the right track for your style of fishing.

To the kayaker who has little serious fishing experience, but would like to learn, you have a distinct advantage. You already enjoy being out there even without the fish. Much of the success in fishing comes with being there at the right time. Read this book. Set up whatever kayak you have now for fishing. Find the right places and learn the right skills and techniques for the species in your area. Continue to enjoy kayaking. Fish will happen. Be attentive to *repeating circumstances*. You will learn.

To potential kayakfishermen that have little fishing experience and have never kayaked, start by kayaking first. It's easy to learn and a lot of fun all by itself. Next, find out what species of fish are in your area. Talk to some local fishermen, especially around tackleshops. Read some books, starting with this one. Who knows, maybe someday you'll take a seakayak tour to Antarctica and flyfish for Coelacanths along the way.

Chapter Two

Why Kayakfish?

For the excitement !

It's fun because it is easy, simple, healthy exercise at your own pace, effective, very exciting, inexpensive and— oh yeah— you get to catch a lot of great fish. Some people do it without the fish. They like to get out in nature and just paddle around. The exercise and nature are the emphasized features, and most of us will admit that we are appreciating those aspects of kayakfishing more than we had anticipated. Kayakfishing is reminiscient of simpler and more economical times when most of us were fishing from canoes or tubefloats rather than our present day floating cadillacs with all of the bells and whistles. The serenity of forest and farm ponds was the emphasized feature, and it was enjoyable with or without the fish. A fishing rod, however, was a required element. Most of us just wish we had somewhere sooner discovered kayaks.

Kayaks are much faster than a speeding tubefloat, but just as relaxing. With a kayak, you can more stealthily stalk the same saltwater flats to watch hooked hundred pound plus tarpon gyrate over your head and crash through the sudsy surface from a perspective that has no comparison by flatsboat. Also, you can get back into the most remote cypress swamp or pond to locate that monster largemouth behind that old moss covered log. You can challenge the surf for a launch at the beach, while your family builds sandcastles, or you can challenge the whitewater of a mountain river to get to those unfished holes full of trout or smallmouth bass. The fun ride can be as good as you'll get at Disneyland. Then there are still the fish and the fishing, and some of the bigger ones will give you quite a ride also.

The real attraction, though, is that it gets you closer to the water, nature, the fish, and the action. Machines do not make things happen. You do. You glide along in a manner that mimics nature itself: quiet, soft, powerful, swift, and efficient. You become impressed with your own ability and a sense of accomplishment. You have become one of nature's most effective predators: independent of the mechanized world. Primitive, and yet— hi-tech. An anachronism that fits. Accepted much more readily by nature's other creatures, you join them in their arena, and they seem to accept you on their terms. The wildlife let you get much closer, even the fish. You may find yourself eyeball to eyeball with giant tarpon that allow you to paddle right into the midst of their school as they gently roll on the glassy, early morning, grass matted surface. All the while, they watch you with an eye seemingly the size of a dinnerplate. Oblivious to your presence, a large herd of redfish charges at you and around your kayak in one foot of shallow, clear water as they chase a school of mullet that jump past your ears in their panic to escape. There are as many thrilling variations as there are environments and species of fish.

Beyond the fun, exercise, excitement, serenity and natural experiences of kayakfishing, there are some definite advantages of fishing by kayak. They are strategic fishing advantages, convenience advantages, and economical advantages. Kayaks will get you back into those inaccessible areas. Kayaks are quieter, espe-

For the advantages !

cially in the shallows where fish are spookier. They are also much quieter in weedy areas where a trolling motor makes a lot of noise and gets hung up in the weeds. Kayaks are faster than the strongest trolling motor which can be very important when you are trying to get quickly to a school of surface breaking fish. Kayaks really outperform trolling motors in weeds where trolling motors are slowed or even become inoperable in heavy vegetation. No other non-motorized craft can take you so far with so little effort, other than a sailboat. Canoes do not even come close to the paddling efficiency of a kayak, especially against the winds and tides. Kayaks give an angler a real freedom to paddle, fish, and explore in confidence and ease. The double bladed paddle laying *at-the-ready* on your lap negates the need to continually be picking up and setting down the paddle carefully to avoid spooking the fish. And with experience, you will learn to paddle forward or backward with one hand while casting, retrieving lures, or fighting fish.

As effective as the strategic advantages are to your fishing, the convenience advantages may actually outweigh them in regards to how many fish you catch. A kayak can be left sitting fully rigged with fishing rods, cooler, tackle etc. and ready to fish in a corner of your garage. In less than a minute, you can slide it into your pickup truck, van, or station wagon and be on your way to the lake. In less than a minute, you are launched. No trailers to mess with and no batteries to charge. Very little cleanup after fishing even in saltwater. There is no engine to flush. You are always ready to go fishing again on short notice. The result is that you actually do go fishing, and as a result, you catch more fish.

If convenience advantages do not get you out fishing more often, perhaps the economical advantages will, since they alone are enough to make you sell your flats or bassboat and buy a kayak. There are so many costs involved with owning a powerboat that most people do not even realize the total expenses. A flatsboat or bassboat fully rigged runs about $17,000 give or take a few thousand and begins depreciating rapidly as soon as you park it in the yard where it sits for too long between fishing trips. (A kayak runs about $800 new and fully rigged.) Then you get into the really sneaky and expensive stuff such as: gas, oil, boat registration, trailer registration, boat insurance, batteries, battery chargers, outboard tune-ups & maintenance, trolling motors, trolling motor repairs, trailer repairs, the dreaded unexpected repairs and my favorite; saltwater corrosion repairs, especially to the wiring. With your kayak, you can say goodbye to all of that stuff and spend more time at some good spots like the one on page 20.

Kayakfishing is not only exciting for the thrills provided by nature, but also because it is a frontier sport. It is a frontier sport because the sport is in the early developmental stages. It is amazing how little information is available. More people are out there doing it, but they are just beginning to communicate it. Writers are just beginning to write about it. There are many kayakers out there, and there are many fishermen. Some of them are beginning to combine the sports to their advantage. Kayakers will often say that they fish a little but are not that skilled or set up that well for fishing. However, many serious fishermen have not yet discovered or considered the kayak as a serious choice of transportation or as a fishing platform. Think of all the wade fishermen out there who could, at the very least, use the kayak to reach new wading areas and to get beyond those unwadable stretches without the hassles of a larger boat. Then consider the added dimension of actually fishing from the kayak itself.

Part of the problem with fishing from a kayak is that until now they had not yet been designed or promoted for sportfishing but for sightseeing, transportation and thrill seeking. The sit-on-top-kayak has been around since about 1971. Some were originally designed for scuba diving, but recently became recognizable as useful for other endeavors such as surf riding and fishing as well as diving. The diving connection led to a better kayak for fishing, since it was designed to be more stable and with increased at-the-ready storage. A few kayakfishermen have discovered this and have begun to make their own additional customizing additions, especially in the area of at-the-ready storage of gear necessary to the sport such as fishing rods and coolers. This birth of an interest in fishing from a kayak has not gone unnoticed by a few manufacturers who now recommend specific models as the best choice for fishermen, and others who have now designed kayaks specifically with fishermen in mind.

Part of the excitement of developing this sport is the type of individuals who gravitate toward it, especially in the beginning stages. They tend to be individualistic, independent thinkers, and they also generally tend to be innovative, educated and computer literate. Among them are some teachers from whom information is getting out about the development of new ideas in epquipment and techniques. There is a need for communication among these early pioneers of the sport, and that vehicle is already in place: the Internet. As ideas and innovations are traded worldwide at a rate unprecedented in recreational pursuits developed in less connected times, the sport is blossoming onto the scene and is being reflected in our sporting and trade magazines seemingly overnight. New techniques and products are becoming available to not only the initial pioneers of the sport, but also, to the swelling ranks of casual to serious kayakfishermen. It probably will never replace or equate with some of our more standard categorizations of fishing, but it is destined to become a fully developed classification with a classic form and with a special class of its own. As the sport develops, hopefully, it will maintain that spirit of kayaking which is simplicity, beauty and independence.

For the good spots !

Chapter Three

Kayakfishing Community &

Communications

Jeff Krieger with 50 lb. halibut

In this new sport, an expert is a relative thing. Many of the most serious kayakfishermen have been at this sport commonly for only about 3 to 4 years. Regardless of skill level, many of these experienced kayakfishermen do not consider themselves experts. But for someone who is just beginning or even just considering the idea, someone with 3 to 4 years experience is a gold mine of information. I would even disagree with some of these individuals and say that, collectively, they are experts, and individually on their own waters—they are the expert. They have a few other things in common. Most importantly, they have an almost fanatical enthusiasm for the sport, a sense of camaraderie, and more important to the reader: an unusually high degree of interest in sharing information and a love of the sport with other potential kayakers.

Paula Clark with a gator seatrout

Many of the top major fishing magazines are now beginning to run magazine articles about the kayakfishing phenomenon and are offering advice and extolling the advantages. Kayak manufacturers that previously considered fishing to be an unrelated sport are now recommending specific models as the best suited for fishermen. Some manufacturers are even designing new models specifically for fishermen. There are new products for and a lot of information coming out about fishing from and rigging kayaks for fishing; also, how to handle the fish you may hook into from this craft. Paddleshops are beginning to add kayakfishing to their lists of available tours and outings. Some long time kayakers are beginning to carry fishing tackle along for the days outing. Veteran fishermen are leaving their high powered boats sit in the garage or are even selling them. Kayakfishing clubs are beginning to form. The greatest factor adding fuel to the fire of this phenomenon, however, is the Internet. Long distance and even international, long term kayakfishing friendships are being formed. The speed at which ideas, experiences, and information are being transferred among the enthusiastic members of this fishing community is unprecedented. There is a collective body of knowledge developing that is a result of a sense of community among kayakfishermen. Many of the *wired* or *connected-to-the-Internet* members of the community are anxious to get the word out to the *unwired* world. What is happening in kayakfishing is nothing short of a revolution.

For those not connected to the Internet, some of the information is beginning to get out there by TV, through local newspaper articles, conventional fishing magazines, even general men's magazines, the first quarterly kayakfishing newsletter, and of course, this book which is the first on the subject at the time of this writing. Recently, a TV fishing host on the Outdoor Life Network recommended a kayak as a fishing vessel. He didn't give a demonstration, but surely one is on the way. Local newspapers are beginning to take notice of local kayak anglers' catches or near catches. Just doing battle with a fish approaching the size of the craft you are fishing from catches the interest of the general public and writers are quick to jump on such a story. Jim Sammons, a California kayakfishing guide, has captured the attention of the *San Diego Tribune*. Ed Zieralski, a staff writer, has written a series of at least three articles chronicling some of Sammons' more adventurous battles. One adventure involved a marlin that towed him eight miles before escaping and other battles with a number of large thresher sharks to 87 pounds in a July 10, 1999 article. The writer seemed to believe that kayakfishing was a quirky California phenomenon, but on the opposite coast a few years earlier *Florida Sportsman Magazine* published a magazine article on kayakfishing. Back in October of 1998 Doug Olander wrote an exciting article for *Sportfishing Magazine* that covered Hawaii and both coasts of the United States. The Coastal Conservation Association's official publication of *Tide Magazine* featured kayakfishing guide Capt. Allen Cartmell of Port O'Connor, Texas in the November-December 1999 issue.

Although his Internet website is probably ground zero for the kayakfishing revolution, probably no one has done more to promote kayakfishing on or off the Internet than Dennis Spike of Coastal Kayak Fishing. He was one of the featured kayakfishermen in the *Sportfishing Magazine* article. He was also featured in *Pacific Fisherman* in July of 1999, *Hooked On The Outdoors Magazine* in August of 1999, and *Men's Journal Magazine* featured him back in March of 1999. Coastal Kayakfishing offers kayakfishing trips off the California coast and Baja waters, gives kayakfishing lessons and clinics, and sells kayfishing accessories; but more importantly here, they publish the *Yak Attack* newsletter. The *Yak Attack* is the only periodical publication devoted solely to kayakfishing. Published quarterly, it is a timely source of kayakfishing information. It has a networking service that allows kayakfishermen from the same area to get in touch with each other. The *Yak Attack* is an excellent way for non Internet users to regularly keep up with developments in the kayakfishing revolution.

Information and education is also getting out to non kayaking fishermen, to non fishing kayakers, and to the general public through kayakfishing guides, paddleshops, kayakfishing tour operators, and even through chance meetings on the water. Guides are one of the most effective means of getting a fast education on kayakfishing. With a guide, you get to spend a whole day picking his brain and receiving one-on-one instructions. Not only that, but you get to see how his whole system works on the water, and you'll probably get to catch some fish. Maybe even a lot of fish. Maybe even a big fish, in which case, you'll get some expert coaching on how to handle the big fish from the kayak. You will get to see, try out, and fish from a professional's kayak of choice, and you will get to see his customizing additions. You may even make a new and valuable life long friend. There is a list of kayakfishing guides in Chapter 17: *Kayakfishing Resources.*

Paddleshops may be able to put you onto a kayakfishing guide in your local area that is not listed in this book. If there are no guides in the area, they may be able to give you the name of a local kayakfisherman with experience. For a few custom tied flies or a few valuable fishing hole secrets, you may be able to weasel your way into getting an on the water demonstration or possibly even a new and experienced kayakfishing buddy. Some paddleshops are more fisher friendly, meaning that they understand the needs of kayakfishermen. The shop may have a fisherman working there or perhaps even the owner is a kayakfisherman. More kayakers and paddleshop owners are taking up kayakfishing everyday.

In 1998, Wade and Paula Clark began paddling and selling kayaks from the *Kayak Korner* of their auction and antique mall in the Port Saint Joe area of the Florida panhandle. A few months after taking up fishing from his kayak, Wade caught a tarpon. Paula has been rewarded with a beautiful *gator* seatrout over 23 1/2 inches long. Wade and Paula have become avid kayak anglers. Wade installs rodholders in his kayaks for his customers and takes potential customers out for demonstration trips. They do not guide or give lessons, but they do occasionally meet with customers to paddle local waters and share all that they can with them. Paula says that kayakfishing has been one of the best activities for their marriage that they have ever shared, and their grandkids show up almost every Sunday for river trips.

David Simms of Action Watersports in Auburndale, Florida is a kayakfisherman and keeps abreast of all the latest accessories and customizing ideas that make kayakfishing efficient and convenient. He will even show you how to install flush mounted rodholders in your kayak. He also has the right rivets, rivet guns, eyelets and straps etc. that you might need to do the job yourself.

Canoesport in Houston, Texas has gone all the way. They have their own kayak hull manufactured in South Carolina, and they customize it for the local fishing area. They call it *The Ultimate Fishing Machine*. A paddleshop in Cayucos, California has their own kayakfishing guides. Known as Cayucos Outfitters, they offer kayakfishing trips on local waters and also give preparatory classes. Some shops, such as: Island Creek Outfitters in Broomes Island, Maryland are beginning to run river kayakfishing float trips catering to those who specifically want to fish. Southwest Paddlesports in Spring, Texas conducts laid back kayakfishing float trips, and describe themselves more as *kayakers who like to fish*. Over at Wilderness Furnishings, Inc. in Sugarland, Texas, the owner often referred to as Pecos Jack, sponsors a kayakfishing club known as P.A.C.K, which stands for *Paddling Anglers in Canoes and Kayaks*. Jerry Blose is the leader of that group and has the most experience on the bays around Houston. If you are in the Houston area and looking for some experienced kayak anglers, check in with Pecos Jack at Wild Furnishing, Inc. and see if you can meet some of the guys in the club. Paddleshops are probably your best bet for finding a kayakfishing club in your area. If you want a complete listing of paddleshops in your area, go to the kayak manufacturers. They usually list the dealers in each state that sell their respective kayaks. Many kayak dealers sell kayaks from different manufacturers. There is also a list of paddleshops in Chapter 17: *Kayakfishing Resources* where kayakfishing is spoken daily.

If you are interested in taking some lessons in kayakfishing, before diving in, there are a number of ways to go. If you feel that you just need a day on the water for some simple instruction, a kayakfishing guide may be able to provide the help you need to get started. Most guides are natural teachers and will often be willing to devote a portion of the day toward instruction. Just remember to adjust your expectations in respect to what you might catch that day since much of the time usually devoted to finding fish will be devoted to instruction. If you want something a little more formal and structured, you may want to enroll in a class or clinic designed to educate you rather than produce great fishing.

If you have enough time to get away, you could attend a multiple day or even a week long clinic that might accomplish both objectives. Coastal Kayak Fishing Clinics can be focused on specific skills such as: using depthfinders or surf launching, but their schools focus on basic kayakfishing skills. Instructional multiple day kayakfishing trips to exotic fishing destinations such as the Sea of Cortez off the Baja peninsula are also available. The accommodations are at Hotel Rancho Leonero. Aside from the instruction, there is plenty of time to fish with the potential to catch big fish: including tuna, pargo, jacks, dorado, roosterfish, and even billfish are possible.

If you want to get a little closer to nature, you can take a week long combination kayaking/flyfishing/camping instructional adventure with Baja Outdoor Activities. The instruction and the trip are lead by Gary Bulla, a master flyfisherman. Gary does the trip for Baja Outdoor Activities and does additional trips himself. Gary also has a marine biologist along on the trip to upgrade everyone's understanding and appreciation for this special environment. He also guides and instructs flyfishing at home in southern California.

As mentioned earlier, some paddleshops are beginning to give kayakfishing instructions as well as offering their guided trips. If you are new to kayaking, paddleshops can help you with kayak selection and paddling. They usually carry a variety of styles and brands. They may be able to demonstrate or allow you to try out specific models. You can even rent a model for a day to be sure that it is the model that you would want to purchase. Some shops will then give you a discount on either the rental or the sale; should you decide to purchase the model. You can also learn much about the accessories such as: backrests, paddles, paddle leashes, paddle clips, and bowlines even if the shop is not oriented toward kayakfishing.

As more and more kayakfishermen are hitting the water, potential kayakfishermen are bumping into them and are becoming influenced to consider kayakfishing. They also gain some invaluable information that helps their beginning efforts to be less experimental. The result is more initial success for new kayak anglers which leads to more enthusiastic kayak anglers to help the next guy. A good example of this process is the entry of Capt. Barry Evans into the sport of kayakfishing. In 1977, Barry got bit by the kayakfishing bug while wading and flyfishing on the Brazos River in north Texas about when he saw a kayakfisherman get out of his kayak and pull it over a shoal that prevented access to a creek. He was also impressed with the kayak's ability to paddle in extremely shallow water. On the Brazos, many of the creeks and creek mouths are shallow, but upstream there are deeper holes holding fish that are inaccessible to most anglers. Barry began to research kayakfishing on the Internet. He also began to observe a few guys in his own flyfishing club who used kayaks at the club's outings. He noticed that they did not struggle with the low water conditions as everyone else did. Even his aluminum canoe could not compare to the performance of the kayaks. He asked some questions and did some further research on the Internet. Then he tried out a few makes and models and decided to purchase a Wilderness Systems' *Ride*. He still has the canoe and a bassboat at home, but given the choice, he takes the kayak every time. Starting at age 59, he has been kayakfishing since 1998. He has added rod holders, a GPS mount system, and paddle clips. He straps a 12 by 24 inch basket into the tankwell of the kayak to hold his anchor, sea anchor, small soft cooler, and extra fly boxes. He mostly flyfishes the Texas rivers and lakes for large-mouth, spotted, white, and striped bass, various panfish, carp, and freshwater drum. In fact, he caught the state record freshwater drum from his kayak. He also occasionally fishes the flats off the Texas coast for redfish and seatrout. Barry is not new to flatsfishing. He was a flats and offshore guide in the Florida Keys during the sixties and seventies. Barry's kayakfishing goals include catching as many species as he can by kayak, and resuming his guide career. This time by kayak.

Internet

Obviously, Barry's positive experience as a beginning kayak-fisherman has been a direct result of chance contact with other kayakfishermen, and perhaps more importantly, his purposeful research on the Internet. In fact, Barry's advice to beginning kayakfishermen is to monitor the kayakfishing websites on the Internet, especially the Coastal Kayak Fishing website. As more and more well educated kayak anglers bump into other fishermen, the whole kayakfishing community's body of general knowledge will be upgraded. The effect is greatly multiplied by the Internet's ability to exchange ideas a little closer to the speed of light.

Tom Stubblefield is a regular on the Coastal Kayak Fishing website's bulletin boards, and he is an accomplished kayakfisherman who does not like to refer to himself as an expert; however, Tom is very knowledgeable on the subject of rigging kayaks, but he attributes his knowledge to other kayakerfishermen who have shared their ideas on the Internet in general and on the Coastal Kayak Fishing bulletin boards in particular. Tom has noted that on some of his visits to the Texas coast he has met kayakfishermen who are not connected to the Internet, and who have never heard of Coastal Kayak Fishing. He says that these guys are really floundering with their efforts to rig and fish from kayaks. Hopefully, they took advantage of their meeting with Tom.

A familiar initial struggle story with a fortunate outcome comes from Mark Ambrozic of Ontario, Canada. Mark did not get the kayakfishing idea from others. Unfortunately, neither did he receive any kayakfishing advice or kayak rigging ideas. It was a solo experiment. Mark recognized the potential of kayaks as fishing craft due to their stealth, maneuverability, portability, and accessibility to weedy, rocky and shallow areas. When he purchased his first kayak, a used sit-on-bottom model, he was impressed with the ease of paddling and his ability to control the craft. However, his first attempt at actually catching a fish was more aptly described as *out of control*. The resulting chaos discouraged Mark from fishing by kayak again that season. Over the winter, Mark designed a system that would safely store two rods, the paddle, and tackle boxes at-the-ready on the front deck of a sit-on-bottom kayak where they could be easily accessed.

Furthermore, it would hold one rod securely in a trolling position. The system was so effective that Mark started selling his system as the *First Mate*, and his new company I.I. Endeavors now has a website on the Internet to promote the kayakfishing *chaos control system* to other sit-on-bottom kayakfishermen.

Mark's website is just one of a wide variety of websites where a kayakfisherman can visit to get kayakfishing products, helpful information or communicate with other kayakfishermen. All of the major kayak companies have websites, and there are a variety of sites where you can locate various kayakfishing accessories. Many paddleshops have their own sites, and some other websites are devoted specifically to kayakfishing, including commercial sites of kayakfishing guides and schools. There are also a number of individuals and clubs that are putting up their own sites for fun and to communicate with other kayakfishermen. Conventional fishing websites occasionally have kayakfishing information and articles posted at their sites. In fact, one of the best articles published on kayakfishing was a feature published on a conventional fishing website. Often, kayakfishing requests for help are answered by referring the individual to one of the kayakfishing sites, usually the Coastal Kayak Fishing website.

Kayak company websites

The websites of the major kayak companies are great resources for kayakfishermen. You can see beautifully illustrated kayaks in various styles, sizes and colors. You can get the technical specifications for each kayak model such as the length, width, weight, and maximum weight capacity. You can get information about the strong points and intended uses of the widely varying models. You can often get the manufacturer's recommended model for kayakfishing. In some cases, you can even get help with rigging specific models of their kayaks for fishing. Heritage Kayaks' website has illustrative photos of Florida flats guide Jackson Reade's customized kayaks and provides a hotlink to his website for kayak anglers to get more information. As kayak companies are becoming more *fisher-friendly*, they are beginning to recommend specific models best suited as a fishing kayak such as the Cobra *Fish and Dive* and Kiwi Kayak's *Stealth*, and now some companies are designing new kayaks specifically for fishing such as the new *Tribalance* kayaks that will allow you to stand up to fish, Ocean Kayak's *Ambush*, and Heritage Kayaks' *Fisherman*. You can also check out many of the accessories for kayaks that are available from their dealers, and you can also locate available dealers and paddleshops in your area. Within their list of paddleshop dealers for their respective kayaks, the kayak company websites usually have hotlinks to the websites of paddleshops that sell their products.

Paddleshop websites

Paddleshop websites vary greatly in content and resources, but they are all helpful. There is a wide variety of useful information to gather there. You can always get useful information on kayaks and accessories. Usually, you can get information about taking lessons or instruction on kayaking or kayakfishing. Often, they will have guides on staff for kayaking and kayakfishing, or in some cases, they have recommendations and contact information for guides listed on their site. Some of them will have a hotlink to the guide's site or an email address. Sometimes the guides will lead group kayakfishing trips from the paddleshop. Some shops sponsor group kayakfishing float trips down local rivers. Their site will often reflect these trips. At some sites of paddleshops that are located on rivers, you can get current river condition information and local maps, including some detailed maps with local fishing tips marked on them. Shenandoah River Outfitters in LuRay, VA. breaks the river down into sections on their website and marks the landings. They also point out the better fishing areas for the bigger fish and where you can catch greater quantities of fish. You can email them to get the current river conditions. Paddleshops and outfitters in popular outdoor recreation areas often will have information at their sites about campgrounds, cabins or other local accommodations.

Fishing guides on the net

Fishing guides are known for their outstanding websites. They are often the best place to go for local fishing information. Many are very forthcoming with free information, and publish seasonal, periodic, weekly, or even daily fishing reports at their site. Some even deliver their fishing reports to you via email if you like. One such guide is Captain Butch Rickey. He does a report for Pine Island Sound on the west coast of Florida. Butch is a kayakfishing guide who runs a very flexible program. If you like, he will just rent you a rigged fishing kayak and point you in the right direction and offer advice. You can also choose to have Butch guide you, but the ultimate service is to have Butch pile the kayaks onto his flatsboat and deliver you and your kayak to the more distant hot fishing locations without the long tedious paddling. Butch has a section of his website that is dedicated to educating visitors to his site about fishing smarter in his neck of the woods. It is free, valuable, top notch information available from a professional to anyone who can point and click on a computer mouse. At Jackson Reade's site, you can get a fishing report for the east coast of Florida, and you can see how his kayaks are rigged for fishing. Of particular interest is his custom solution for a livewell behind the seats of his Aquaterra *Prism* kayaks. Jackson also goes into great detail about the flatsfishing environment of the Intercoastal Waterway, Indian River Lagoon, the Banana River No-Motor-Zone, and the Merritt Island National Wildlife Refuge. The Internet is truly amazing. On the same night that you explore both coasts of the Florida peninsula with Captain Butch Rickey and Jackson Reade, you can surf on over to the Baja peninsula to go kayak flyfishing in the Sea of Cortez with Gary Bulla or learn how you can take a kayakfishing lesson with Dennis Spike of Coastal Kayak Fishing.

The Coastal Kayak Fishing Website is more than a guide's website. It is the mother of all kayakfishing sites. At the site, you can get information about kayakfishing trips to Baja waters or off the California coast, get information about schools and clinics, read informative feature articles on selected kayakfishing topics, sign up for the *Yak Attack* newsletter, learn about and purchase kayakfishing accessories that make the the sport a workable concept, but most important of all, you can communicate with other kayakfishermen from all over the continent on the bulletin boards. On the bulletin boards, you can get an education or just plain conversation with like minded kayakfishermen. If you have a question about kayakfishing or fishing in another part of the country, you can toss it out there for everyone or anyone to express their opinion or expertise. Conversing and communicating on the boards are some very knowledgeable kayakfishermen who are just as enthusiastic about helping *newbies* as they are about practicing their sport.

Kayakfishing friends on the net

Tom Stubblefield, mentioned previously, is a great example of the kayakfishermen you can meet on the web. Tom is a self proclaimed web educated kayakfisherman. He attributes most of what he has learned to other kayakfishermen he has met on the web. He hangs out on the bulletin boards at the Coastal Kayak Fishing website. Tom is a registered pharmacist. He grew up fishing out of canoes. He then graduated to bassboats, and he spent more than a few years at tournament fishing. Tom says that his days as a jet jockey in a powerboat are over. He's now more interested in his health and in getting closer to nature. Rather than competing in tournaments, he prefers to share the joys of kayakfishing with other kayakfishermen which he considers to be a special breed. Tom says the fanaticism of the kayakfishing crowd cuts through all social and financial classes, and yields a camaraderie that lends itself to the generous sharing of information. When he gets together with others that share his appreciation for these efficient, self-propelled craft, they generally compare each others' ideas and improvements to their craft. Rigging kayaks is Tom's particular specialty. Tom paddles an Ocean Kayak *Scupper Pro T/W* with a movable anchor system, rod holders, depthfinder, GPS, and all the tackle storage needed for a day or even a weekend of fishing. He is even rigged for night fishing, and his lime green kayak will light up from the inside and glow in the dark. If you don't catch up with Tom on the water, you can reach him at the Gulf Coast bulletin boards on the Coastal Kayakfishing website. Look for postings by TStubb/Texas, or you can email Tom directly at tstubb@hotmail.com.

One of Tom's regular friends on the web is Vivian Oliva. Vivian is the owner of a window treatment company that specializes in high end residential work. Her company caters to designers and architects. On the water, Vivian paddles the Everglades National Park in search of snook, redfish, seatrout, grouper, snapper, pompano, mackerel, tripletail, and cobia. The snook are her favorite. Vivian's more notable kayak snook catches have measured between 36 to 42 inches in length, and redfish catches between 27 to 36 inches. Since taking up kayakfishing, she no longer uses any live bait. She likes soft plastic artificials but sometimes uses bucktails and spoons. She throws the lures on a ten pound line spinning outfit with a Daiwa BG 13 spinning reel and a medium/heavy Falcon rod. Her favorite methods are jigging and trolling when she's traveling a long way. In her efforts to learn more about the large area that she fishes, she takes many extended six day kayakfishing/camping trips to extend her range. Her favorite kayak is the Ocean Kayak *Scupper Pro* with a center hatch, twin hatches and a rudder, because it can accommodate the camping gear and because of the model's stability, speed, and seaworthiness. She is also pleased with the incredible customer service at Ocean Kayak. Vivian has added a couple of flushmounted rodholders behind the seat, an anchoring system, a pliers sheath in front of the center hatch, and a paddle clip forward of the cockpit to hold her landing net that sits on top of her forward hatch. She recommends that new kayakfishermen try out a variety of models to find the kayak that is right for them.

Vivian fished out of a powerboat for 16 years, but sold it to buy a kayak as a way to get more exercise. On her first trip, she was stunned by how silently she approached the fish and wildlife without spooking them. She caught more fish and had more fun doing it. She feels that kayakfishing is better for the body, soul, the environment and her pocketbook. Her main goals for the future are to learn more about the areas she fishes by fishing different tides, seasons, and moon phases. She also wants to take a one way trip from Everglades City to Flamingo, fishing and trolling the entire 99 mile Wilderness Waterway. You can check on Vivian's progress at the Coastal Kayakfishing bulletin boards, which she highly recommends, or email her directly at snook@gate.net.

The CKF boards have been so popular that other bulletin board sites are beginning to pop up on the net. Yakfishing.com is another bulletin board website where there are no lessons, services, trips or products for sale. Just lots of kayakfishermen and potential kayakfishermen exchanging information. One major plus for this site is that Jim Sammons of La Jolla Kayak Fishing, who is an experienced kayakfishing guide, hangs out at this site and is available as a source of experience and expertise. Mark Hunter owns the site and provides it as a service to the kayakfishing community. He is also an experienced and knowledgeable kayakfisherman and a frequent contributor to the group conversation.

It is interesting to note that more kayakfishing websites by individuals or groups of individuals are beginning to appear on the net with no profit motive. The individuals who host the sites simply love kayakfishing and sharing their love for the sport, their experiences, and their expertise with other kayak anglers or potential converts. The best example of this development is the Extreme Kayak Fishing website hosted by the three amigos of kayakfishing: *SSRedfish*, *Great ExSPECKtations*, and *Flounder Pounder*. They are otherwise known as Sean Smith, Kevin Olmstead and Jake Markris. Apparently, Sean Smith was the spearhead for the group into the kayakfishing adventure. Sean wanted to buy a kayak to tap the potential of seatrout and redfishing in Alabama's Mobile Bay. Kevin Olmstead soon joined into Sean's adventure after hearing the wild success stories from his initial experiences. The contagion spread when Kevin returned from the mutual adventures equally wild eyed from the fishing success. Jake soon after accompanied Sean and you can read about his initial fantastic kayakfishing trips at their new mutual website where Jake shares his take on the group's experiences. They have opened the site up to all fellow kayakfishermen to share their photos and kayakfishing experiences with all who visit their site. In fact, they have solicited input about the future objectives and direction of the site from fellow kayakfishers. A quick read of the incoming mail posted on the site reveals a hearty approval of their efforts, enthusiasm and plans for their site.

You can meet some very interesting kayakfishermen at their site. George Whillock is one of the first visitors to post photos there. One look at the photos will reveal two things about George. He is a terrible photographer and a great fisherman. Just kidding about the photography. Not many kayak anglers are as able or willing to catch, pull on board and photograph the large blacktip sharks that George has caught all by himself in his kayak (see page 210). George doesn't gaff the sharks that he does not want to eat. He pulls them up by the tail after tiring them down fully. It works pretty well on the blacktips, but the sand sharks try to whip around and bite when seized by the tail.

George has had some amazing success at kayakfishing very quickly. George was a pier fisherman at the Gulf State Pier in Alabama. Unfortunately, siltation from the last several hurricanes has caused the depth at the pier to go from 20 ft. to 12 ft., causing the cobia to pass by the pier further out of reach more often than in the past seasons. George could see the boats a half a mile southeast of the pier catching cobia, and he had heard that guys on the west coast were fishing out of kayaks. Fishing for only a couple months of this past spring and summer from his new *Scupper Pro* from Ocean Kayak, he has caught jack crevalle, redfish, bonito, king mackerel, blacktip and sand sharks. George attributes his immediate success to his ability to apply his pier fishing experience to kayakfishing. His reliance on the use of live bait is probably also a major factor. George will make great efforts to catch the best live bait that he can obtain and keep it lively. He prefers 5 inch menhaden, locally referred to as *l-ys*, but he will also use small croakers or pinfish as a last resort.

George uses a simple 5 gallon bucket as a livewell with a trap door lid. He drills holes in the sides of the bucket except for the last four to five inches. He has to repeatedly stop to refresh the water in the bottom of the bucket while paddling, but he sets it overboard for continuous water exchange upon reaching the fishing area. George has had some problems with big fish swinging around and tangling his anchor rope, and he is now using a quick release anchor system, but he is not completely satisfied with the results. He does not like the long distance drifting uncertainties while battling a large fish even with a drift chute out. His concerns are understandable since he is shooting for a 50-60 lb. cobia and a 30 lb. king mackerel. George had an unusual experience when his paddle leash failed, and he had to make the decision to jump overboard into his own shark inhabited chum slick to retrieve the paddle before it drifted any further away. He now carries an extra paddle onboard. If you want to trade ideas with George, you can email him at jorge@zebra.net.

Occasionally, you can pick up some valuable kayakfishing information on conventional fishing websites. Of course, they always have valuable fishing information at these sites, but one of the best and most informative kayakfishing articles is published on the Stripersurf.com website. The article is entitled *East Coast Kayak Fishing*, and it was written by Ken Sigvardson. He is a director of a pharmaceutical company, but if you spend some time talking with him, you will think that he is a guide. He is that knowledgeable and experienced. Ken has been kayakfishing since 1996. He is now from Delaware, but he grew up and still fishes the northeast coast from New Jersey, to Montauk Point, and especially around Cape Cod and Martha's Vineyard. Although he fishes the Chesapeake Bay near his new home, he is more than willing to drive 8 hours to fish the northeast coast. The reason he likes the area so much is the remoteness of many of the surf fishing areas. It is a long trip by boat to some of them, and beach access requires a four wheel drive to get to the more remote sections. The result is less fishing pressure. Striped bass are the prize, but bluefish and false albacore are a bonus. Ken doesn't go surf fishing without a couple of kayaks strapped to the roof of his 4WD. He needs an extra kayak now because his son, Derek, is now also a kayakfishing fanatic. Derek has caught one of those finicky but hard fighting false albacore weighing in at 12 pounds.

Kayakfishing fever is spreading. One of Ken's best fishing buddies has also purchased a kayak. You can read more about Ken, his adventures and advice to kayakfishermen in Chapter 16: *Kayakfishing Experts.* You can contact Ken by email at sigvark@attglobal.net.

Derek Sigvardson with a false albacore

In addition to kayakfishing and conventional fishing websites, there are also many useful miscellaneous sites on the Internet. Some of the most useful involve services for obtaining information on tides and weather. You can also view or download a variety of map options from such sites as MapQuest and MapBlast. One of the most unusual, unique and useful sites to any outdoorsman, however, is the Microsoft Terraserver website. At this site, you can view for free or download satellite, aerial, and topographical maps for a charge. Particularly exciting are the satellite maps where you can eventually zoom in close enough to almost make out individual trees in a forest or visibly check the depth on a pond.

Although you can get a lot of great information on the web, it is the people you meet that really make the Internet great for kayakfishermen. While searching for experienced kayakfishermen on the net, I met Matt Fuller from Sealy, Texas. Matt, typically, did not want to be considered an expert but wanted to be of help to my efforts to write the book and was apologetic for having only *limited* experience and being of a youthful age. As a Texas A&M student, he has found the time to get more experience in both saltwater flatsfishing and freshwater fishing than most of us will ever achieve, but that's not what will make you envious about Matt. Matt bought a kayak after an encounter with a kayak fisherman on a freshwater creek. He bought it to access the shallow waters, also because it was much lighter than his family's jonboats and canoes, and because he wanted a new toy. In saltwater, Matt fishes Matagorda Bay, Oyster Lake, Caney Creek, Wolf Island, Chinapin Point, Christmas Bay, Brown Cedar Bay, Mad Island and the San Bernard River. He uses mostly plastic touts for seatrout and flounder, and he sometimes flyfishes for redfish, but that might not make you jealous of Matt.

Actually, Matt prefers freshwater fishing by kayak. He likes throwing topwater plugs for bass because the low perspective from the kayak makes it more exciting down nearer to the fish's level. He has many opportunities right near his home such as the Brazos River, the Colorado River, La Grange, Bastrop, and the San Bernard which is a small but excellent crappie river and only one mile from his house. He also fishes Lakes Sommerville, Texana, and Lake o' the Pines, but his favorites are the small tributary creeks coming off of the rivers because they are shallow and inaccessible without a canoe or a kayak. However, these small creeks hold some big fish in the upstream deeper holes. He likes Mill Creek on the Brazos River, and Piper's and Redgate creeks on the Colorado River. He particularly likes Cummins Creek where he caught his biggest bass of approximately 8 lbs. Matt has caught a number of bass in the 8lb class. Now, that *might* make you jealous.

All of Matt's personal best catches of largemouth bass, crappie, catfish, seatrout, and flounder have come by kayak. He is still working on his biggest redfish. Matt paddles an Aquaterra

Prism. Matt has customized his kayak with rodholders, a cooler, a fish ruler, a compass and deck bunji rigging. Matt has some advice for beginning kayakfishermen. He says that space organization is the key. Try to have all the supplies you need ready to handle a fish and place the fish in a basket, cooler or stringer without actually bringing the fish onboard. He says you don't want sharp toothed seatrout or spike finned catfish bouncing around on your lap.

Matt also bowfishes from his kayak and usually winds up in the creek after shooting a big gar. Now, a sage word of advice from *Eskimo Joe* about not shooting sharp primitive objects at creatures larger than the kayak. Just kidding, Matt. What makes you really jealous of Matt is not all of the valuable experience and the exciting experiences he has had so far, but rather, all of the experience he is going to gain in the next 60 years of kayakfishing. All in agreement say, *aye*. Why did we wait so long?

Remember Capt. Barry Evans, the retired Florida fishing guide and born again kayakfisherman from earlier in the chapter? Wouldn't it be neat if Matt was the guy Barry spotted sneaking back up into that creek off the Brazos River that lead to Barry's new kayakfishing career? Wouldn't it be neat if after reading this book, they emailed each other and became kayakfishing buddies? You can reach Matt for help and advice at his email address: fullertamu@hotmail.com.

Fishing is such an inexact science, and kayakfishing is even more so. With various species of fish in environments where no two sets of conditions are exactly the same, various tackle, techniques and an endless variety of lures used in conventional and nonconventional manners, throw in the human imagination, and no one kayak is the perfect kayak for all situations or for every angler. No lure or technique is the ultimate or correct choice for each new day or every environmental situation, not even for one species. In fact, the best choices and combinations are probably yet to be discovered, at least, for each new day. It is the possibilities that make each new day unique. It is the anticipation of the unknown possibilities that make fishing fun. One mind can only imagine, consider and calculate so many of the possibilities. Thinking, creating, experimenting, and communicating collectively will hurl kayakfishing to the forefront of the sportfishing scene, and create greater choices and possibilities for all of us. It will also be a lot more fun.

Chapter Four

Where To Kayakfish

Mountain streams

Because kayaks are so versatile, there are almost no limitations to your choices of where you can fish with them. You can fish wherever fish swim. On the macro scale you can use maps to choose between oceans, bays, rivers, streams, lakes, ponds, or swamps. You can choose fresh or saltwater. Inland or offshore. Shallow or deep. Wide open spaces with big sky horizons or hidden and remote places. You can paddle and fish an ocean via a surf launch one day and four wheel drive to a backwoods swamp paddle the next day from the same kayak. You might choose the serene, still water of a quiet pond in the early morning or an evening. On another day, you may decide for the excitement of a refreshing downstream whitewater challenge to cast at oppurtunities usually presenting themselves as trout, salmon or smallmouth bass behind many numerous rocks or in quiet pools along the way. Other moving waters could be tidal estuaries where the water levels, speed, and direction of the water flow is dependent upon the moon phase and position as it revolves around the earth, and where fishing success and strategy are closely tied with the daily tidal changes. The brackish water areas of these tidal creeks are especially interesting because you might catch a fresh or saltwater fish in this area. You never know which will attack your lure next. The decisions are yours. Your only limits are your own desires and abilities.

Gulf of Mexico island catch

Deciding where to fish is a process that involves what type of fish you want to catch, the type of environment you want to experience, how you want to fish for them and what size fish you want to catch. A good single species example is the striped bass. Obviously, since it is most often considered to be a saltwater species, the ocean is a good place to start. But stripers are an anadromous species which means that they run upstream into freshwater where rivers and creeks can be relatively small and still hold sizeable populations of stripers, especially when they are on their spring spawning run. At times the fish upriver may even be larger than the fish you will catch in the ocean. Stripers have also been stocked into many landlocked lakes where they often attain weights that challenge the ocean and estuarial fish.

Saltwater feeding frenzy

In each environment, there are differing techniques, lures and baits that are most effective for catching them. Though there are many generalities, each watershed environment has its own peculiarities. The kayaker seeking stripers has a wide range of paddling environments to seek this adversary. The larger fish of many species often hang out in separate environments than the younger fish of the species, and catching schoolie stripers crashing bait on the surface is not the same game as live-lining a herring or eel for a 35 to 65 pounder (see Chapter 12: *Kayak Live Bait Fishing*). At times in some rivers, a small piece of bloodworm will catch more and larger stripers than the live baitfish. Live baitfish are more difficult to obtain and harder to keep alive and fresh while fishing from a kayak. For a kayaker, what to catch is not only a decision of which species, but also, what size of the species. In a kayak, some forethought and planning are required when hunting fish almost as large as the craft you are fishing from, especially if you are planning to get a picture or take the creature home. I will refer the reader to the chapters on *Kayak Fish Fighting*, *Kayak Fish Handling*, and *Kayakfishing Safety* at this point and move on.

Gary Bulla flyfishing off the Baja peninsula

With many fishermen, the decision of what to catch is probably the first and most important consideration. From there they will decide where and how to fish and even what type of boat and tackle to use. But for a kayakfisherman, sometimes the environment is more important than the species to be caught: not because of any limitations of the kayak but because of the versatility of kayaks and the preference of an individual kayaker on a given day with so many varied oppurtunities. Some trout fishermen prefer big wide rivers, and others enjoy the intimacy of a smaller creek or brook. The choices will vary. It is a matter of emphasis. Catching one good fish in the surroundings you prefer can be more satisfying than ten fish in another setting. When the fishing in your chosen favorite environment is hot, it just doesn't get any better.

Sometimes where you fish depends upon how far you have to paddle. Other times, it's a matter of how far you want to paddle, how much time you have, or your ability to paddle. Kayaking is great exercise, and age is rarely a barrier to the sport although

Flyfishing for schoolie stripers in Florida

physical conditioning and health might be. Still, kayaking is very popular with octogenarians.

Regardless of the reasons, short paddling distances or lack of sufficient time need not limit fishing success. Fishing smarter will catch you more fish than fishing harder and paddling further almost every time. Good planning can make up for a lack of paddling ability or time available. Always use a map when fishing areas that you do not know so well. If possible, pick a launch site that will give a high probability of catching fish close to the launch areas. Choose a route that will present the most oppurtunity along the way. Travel a circular route that will give you as many fishy oppurtunities on the way back to the ramp as on the way out. If possible, plan to be at the fishiest spots at the peak fishing times. Consider the winds, and how they will effect your progress and your fishing efficiency. Evaluate whether to fish the leeward shore or to use the wind to drift fish. Learn to use winds to raise your fishing efficiency (see Chapter 9: *Kayakfishing Skills and Techniques*). Harness the wind to save time and energy. Bass

Ken Sigvardson's big striped bass off the northeastern coast

fishermen all know that warm fronts with southerly winds mean biting bass and cold fronts mean that the fish will shut off. But just before and sometimes just as the cold front hits, the bass usually bite the best. Try fishing your way north with the southerly wind at your back. You can fish efficiently with a minimum of paddling on the way out. Then, when the wind switches, fish your way back south with the northerly wind. Be careful where and when you use this trick because cold fronts often trigger strong winds and storms. I use this trick regularly on a large lake where the water is so shallow that you could easily walk home, and there is literally no chance of drowning. Some kayakfishermen take an umbrella out with them to shade them from the afternoon sun, and when the afternoon seabreeze kicks in, they use it as a sail to hitch a free ride back to shore. You can sometimes use a large bladed paddle as a mast and sail to harness a little wind power while you are resting from paddling.

Where to fish often depends upon *when* you are planning to fish. Timing is everything. You can be in the right place doing the

Rich Torgun's New Jersey pond bass

right thing and nothing may happen if you are there at the wrong time. Determining the right time is a matter of probability that is specific to a species of fish, and most often specific to an environment. It can be evaluated in terms of weather, moon phases, tidal flows, major feeding or activity periods (solunar periods), time of day, time of season or any other individual situational factor with repeating circumstances that yields an oppurtunity to predict fishing success.

Probably one of the best known and predictable effects of weather upon feeding behavior of fish is the infamous cold front, and its resultant lockjaw effect on largemouth bass. Some of the best bass fishing occurs just before the cold front hits while the weather is still warm. As an example of weather and predictable fish feeding behavior in a smaller localized situation, consider a small central Florida coastal spring creek which explodes with a multiple species feeding binge whenever a tropical storm or un-

White seabass off the California coast

usually heavy thunderstorms raise water levels about a foot with a heavy outflow. Since about half of this 8 mile creek is tidal, the high tide and heavy rain combine to increase high water and increase outflow on outgoing tide. Under these circumstances, saltwater fish will move up into the usually shallow clear springwater sections and join the usually wary bass population in an all out feeding binge.

Moon phases can have direct and indirect effects on feeding or activity periods. Full moons, new moons, quarter moons and their fractional periods in between all have their well documented influences on many species of fish in varying ways. Also the daily position of the moon, as the earth rotates on its axis, contributes along with the sun to the well published *solunar tables* that predict daily feeding and intra-day *activity periods*. The moon is also responsible for tides in tidal areas. Tides will affect different species of fish in differing environments in various ways.

Often the same species will act differently toward tidal stages in differing environments in the same general area. On the Gulf

Colin Harrison with a Canadian largemouth bass

coast of Florida, there are two groups of tarpon that are only a few miles apart. The first school feeds on early morning, low water, incoming tides in an area of intermingling channels and islands with shallow flats. The second group appears suddenly at flood tide on the surface when it occurs between 10:00 AM and 2:00 PM and disappears about two hours later. They are very dependable year after year. The launch site is between each location. Therefor, the direction to paddle depends on the time of day and the tide. Also, you would not even go there for tarpon except during that two and a half month season they spend in the area.

There is a beautiful trout stream full of fish that runs through a small canyon in north central Pennsylvannia. It is one of the most beautiful trout streams full of fish that you will ever find, but you wouldn't want to fish it unless there was a chance that your trip would coincide with the peak of the infamous *Green Drake Mayfly hatch*. At that time, those wary old trout turn into giddy school kids at an old fashioned penny scramble. Snook around docks are often difficult to catch, but at night around lighted docks, they often lose their caution. Many other species fall for the lights at night trick. These are just a few examples that *where* you fish is also a matter of *when*.

Gulf of Mexico blacktip shark

So, there are a lot of factors to be considered when considering where to go kayakfishing. In order to raise your odds for success, there are two main pieces of advice. One, try to put together as many positive factors as you can into your decision of when to go where. My favorite example is about a big bass I once caught on a flyrod much too long ago, but the memory and details are still fresh. It was bass spawning season in central Florida, and I was on the lookout for oppurunities to catch some bigger bass on my flyrod. It was February which is a choice spawning month. It was three days before the full moon which is a prime feeding period when the weather cooperates. A week long warm front of 88 degrees was about to collide with an approaching cold front. I didn't have a guide client that day. I was working on some fish mounts in my taxidermy shop. It was about twenty minutes until the published major feed period. I knew a deep gator hole in a large shallow grass prairie pond in the Ocala National Forest that was rarely fished. It has many big fish, and it was about five minutes from my house. I couldn't stand it. I dropped my taxidermy tools and grabbed my flyrod. Twenty minutes and one cast later I had my hands on the lower jaw of a 12 lb. 4 oz dream. It was 5 ounces shy of the flyrod world record at that time.

The second piece of advice would be to develop your multiple species versatility. Learn the positive and negative influences on the fish in your area. Learn the effects of weather, moon influences, and seasons on the species and environments you kayakfish. Always be mindful of potential repeating circumstances. Try to discover new situations and predict their reoccurence. Adjust thinking where necessary. Try to develop a strategy that will put you at the best places to catch the species with the highest probability of success for the weather and other enviromental factors on that day. On the other hand, kayakfishing is fun even without the fish. So, fish where and when you want, and enjoy it.

Where you fish will effect *the way you fish* and might have an effect on what kayak accessories, fishing epquipment, or even which kayak style and model you need. You can develop a vertical or horizontal style of fishing. Vertical style fish hunting is practiced in relatively deeper water and your hunt sometimes involves some hitech epquipment such as electronic depthfinders or fishfinders but not always. In a more horizontal style of fish-

finding, your depthfinder is more often the end of your fishing
pole or your kayak paddle, and your fishfinders are your eyes,
ears, and fishing lures. Vertical fishing involves longer anchor
ropes and possibly anchor cranking aids. Horizontal fishing involves sightfishing and stealth. The highest technology is probably invested in your graphite rod or your polarized sunglassess.
Your anchor rope is probably shorter than your kayak.

   If you want to hunt for bass in heavy weedcover, then you
will want to use heavy tackle and learn to fish frog imitations
slowly over the lily pads, or buzzbaits steadily over the top, but
one of the most effective methods is flipping. In flipping, you do
not cast and retrieve; instead, you use a long rod much like a cane
pole to place a sinking plastic worm into pockets among the weeds,
hopefully dropping it right on the nose of a big bass (see Chapter
11 *Kayak Lure Fishing*). Flipping is especially effective from a
kayak due to a kayak's stealth factor. One of the most effective
big bass techniques is to slowly troll along the weed edge with
large live golden shiners which requires heavy tackle and a system of keeping the fragile shiners alive (see Chapter 12: *Kayak*

Snook in the mangroves

Live Bait Fishing). If you like fishing beautiful trout streams, then you might want to use a flyrod. A flyrod would also be a good choice on smallmouth bass rivers. If you want to fish for snook around mangroves, then you probably should use a bigger flyrod with a stronger tippet to force bigger fish away from roots. When fishing rivers or lakes with log strewn bottoms, you may need to change your anchor to a dragging chain that will slide over and not hang up on the logs. If you want to launch or return in the surf, you may want to install a set of paddle clips or other means of locking down your rods in the event of an overturned kayak. In open waters, you may want to attach a sea anchor to control drift (see Chapter 9: *Kayakfishing Skills and Techniques*). If you plan to do a lot of paddling in wide open waters, especially for longer distances, you may want to use a longer kayak for more efficient paddling. If you plan to hop around from pond to pond, you may want a smaller kayak that will be less work to handle and launch. If versatility is your goal, then you will want a mid-size kayak that is wide and more stabile (see Chapter 5: *Choosing a Kayak*). You may want to own more than one kayak.

Chapter Five

Choosing A Kayak

Ken Sigvardson in his *Pachena* from Current Designs

Before buying a kayak, ask yourself the following questions. Where are you likely to fish? What are you likely to fish for? How are you likely to fish for them? Consider whether you will fish only in your local area or also travel to unexpected destinations. Try to determine if you will fish in freshwater or saltwater. If you will fish in freshwater, think about how often you will fish small ponds, larger lakes, streams or big rivers. In saltwater, consider whether you will be fishing backwaters, bays, or launching in the surf. Identify your target species. Will it be big game or bluegills? Will you use live bait, artificial lures, or flyfish? If you know where you are likely to fish, what you are likely to fish for, and how you are likely to fish for them, then it will be a simple matter to choose a kayak from the many styles and manufacturers based on the following considerations: paddling ability, stability, maneuverability, wading ability, storage capacity, fishability, transportability, affordability, comfort, and the ability to test or tryout. These considerations should be used as general guidelines to help you evaluate whether a kayak model will be right for your fishing pursuits.

Paddle-ability

Transportation is the number one function of a kayak. Any kayak is an efficient mode of transportation. There are varying degrees of efficiency of transport among the kayak clan. The degrees of efficiency are modified by the variables of the kayak's design and the environment to be navigated. However, in the nonmotorized class of vessels, kayaks blow away the competition with the exception of sailboats, and there are again, some hybrid models of kayaks are capable of mounting a sail, but let's avoid further digression. Kayaks paddle better than canoes, especially *into the wind*. Other rowing craft are generally cumbersome and less simplistic. There are other forms of transportation that are simpler and more convenient and even more economical: such as a tubefloat, but when it comes to transportation, it boils down to which kayak. At this point, we have to ask how far we are going to transport, under what environmental conditions, and when we get to where we are going, what do we need from the kayak to aid our fishing? Beyond that, do we expect to travel and fish repeatedly through and to the same situations, or will we be traveling and fishing variable environmental conditions and fishing situations?

These are critical considerations in the choosing of a kayak. The answers to these questions will determine how much emphasis you put on transportation or paddle-ability versus the remaining considerations. Let's look at some examples. On the west coast, there is a group of enthusiastic kayakers that launch in the surf and paddle out to the kelp beds to fish for a variety of fish, especially kelp bass that are attracted to these offshore grassbeds. Much of the fishing is straight down, often fishing through small openings in the weed cover, especially on days when the fish are holding tight to cover. Some guys are even mounting depthfinders on their kayaks to help them find fish, especially when fishing away from the visible cover. Contrast that with a Florida saltwater flatsfisherman who traverses relatively calm shallow water and does most of his fish probing toward the horizon rather than below. The flatsfisherman may not have the objective of an offshore kelp bed to which he will often fish all day and will not have to launch in and land in a challenging surf. He may, however, do a lot of traveling and paddling in the course of a day, and he may or may not actually fish out of the kayak. He may use the kayak to reach the shallow grassflats and then get out and wade, especially if he is a flyfisherman. Now consider a river or stream fisherman, particularly on waters with at least some whitewater. Again this fisherman may wade when reaching strategic sections of the river or may fish entirely from the kayak or a combination of both. Knowing your paddling environment and your objectives will help you decide between the many kayak styles, and where you may need to trade off some paddling efficiency for other considerations such as stability, fish-ability, maneuverability, storage capacity, or transportability.

Some more expensive kayak designs attempt to maximize paddling efficiency while retaining a higher degree of stability. These designs utilize a feature termed *secondary stability* where the lower portion of the kayak that rides at or below the water surface is more narrow for paddling efficiency. However, a wider area of the kayak rides above the water surface, reducing contact with the water. As the kayak lists or leans on the water surface, the wider portion begins to contact the water surface, creating a buoying effect and stabilizing the kayak. The result is a kayak that at first seems tippy but is secondarily, actually more stabile. This style of kayak design is a favorite of kayakfishing experts Ken Sigvardson and Rick Roberts. Ken fishes the northeast coast for stripers from his *Pachena* sit-on-bottom model from Current

Designs. However, Ken usually recommends the *Acadia* model from Perception Kayaks to beginners because it is cheaper, but also because it is wider and more initially stabile. Rick Roberts, however, always recommends the superior secondary stability design of the Heritage Kayaks models to increase paddling efficiency.

illustration #1

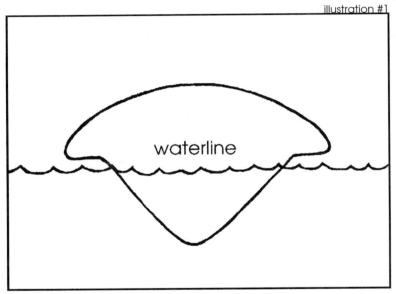

Secondary stability design

Stability

Stability is the number one trade off for speed & paddling efficiency of kayaks. You want stability in a fishing kayak. Doing eskimo rolls has no tactical fishing advantages unless: you are wearing goggles, insist on knowing what the fish are doing, and do not want the frills of installing a fishfinder. Stability will help you launch in the surf and return safely with all of your gear that you went out with. It will help you navigate that whitewater stretch to reach those unfished honeyholes. It will make your kayak more maneuverable. It will allow you to move around in your kayak to reach gear, fight fish, change your position to fish, or just relax while hanging your feet over the side. It will make your kayak more comfortable and allow you to spend more time in it per day. In some kayaks, it will even allow you to stand and fish which is especially helpful when sightfishing. It will allow you to climb overboard to wade fish and easily reboard when needed. Wading can drastically increase your fish catching potential in many situations. Stability can increase storage capacity and convenience. Stability comes from width and width will allow you to store more gear with increased freedom of storage positioning to enhance fishing convenience. So, stability will actually enhance most all of the the additional considerations, other than efficiency of paddling. Stability will increase your kayak's fishability. The best question for some kayakers may be—how much stability are you willing or do you need to give up for more speed and paddling efficiency? Kayaks with the recommended stability for kayakfishing have a hull width of about 26 - 30 inches. Kayaks with more paddling efficiency have hull widths of about 22-24 inches.

Maneuverability

Maneuverability is a result of length, hull design, and to a lesser extent, width. The longer the kayak, the slower the turn. The flatter the bottom, the easier to turn. A keel on the bottom resists turning. The deeper the keel, the more the resistance. In some models, the keel can be built into the bow and aft sections of the kayak rather than the bottom of the kayak. If a portion of the kayak's bow or aft cuts sharply below the surface, especially if it comes to a sharp point, then it will resist turning. So length and hull design can limit maneuverabilty. Kayak designers purposely limit maneuverability in some designs to achieve the result of a kayak that *tracks true* which means that it stays on course while paddling. Wind, water movement and inefficient paddling will not have as much effect on its course underway. That means it will be more efficient at getting from point A to point B. Less energy will be required to correct course and more energy will be directed at forward movement. *True tracking* is great when you are paddling a long way, especially if there is a crosswind or current. Even a strong tail wind can continually throw you off course by blowing against your body and your cooler on the aft section of your kayak. Sometimes wind and water conditions are so extreme, however, that continual correction is required. True tracking *resists* correction. That is why many big water touring kayaks add a *rudder*. With a rudder, you do not have to expend undue energy correcting course on a true tracking designed kayak. In confused or quickly changing water conditions such as whitewater, surf or stormy conditions, forward movement is not the only concern. Quick corrections and stability are needed. A rudder would not be enough. Shorter, wider kayaks with flatter bottoms excel in these conditions.

So, what does this mean to a fisherman? Where do you draw the line between true tracking and maneuverability? It depends upon your fishing environment. Generally speaking, if you are going to paddle a long way in open water to a generally wide area with no specific pinpointable targets and especially if you are going to anchor over deep water or drift the area, you may not need a more maneuverable kayak. You want keels and length if you are going the distance, and you want enough stability to do what you need to do to catch fish, handle the fish and to be comfortable. If you are not going to paddle so far, then more stability would be beneficial. You may even paddle a long way but then get out of the kayak to fish. Stability and access to epquipment become less of a factor to consider. You will however, depending upon the depth, need enough stability to exit and enter your craft. If it is waist deep or higher, you will need more stability than if it is knee to ankle deep. Consider depth fluctuations due to wind, weather and tides in your planning.

Your fishing situation may require more maneuverability if you will be casting to visible targets, especially in situations where you are moving along with the wind, tide or downstream current. Shoreline casting to targets such as beneath overhanging trees, downed logs, lily pads and docks can be complicatd by a wind that wants to blow you into the target or away from it. Downstream currents can be tricky and not only prevent you from casting to shoreline line logs and rocks, they may threaten you with collisions on rocks or force you underneath overhanging trees and vine-like entanglements. Tidal currents can deceptively move you away from or suddenly on top of your casting targets such as sandbars, rocks or oyster bars. Oyster bars are not friendly to kayak bottoms. They gouge long cuts through the polyethylene and fibreglass. You can scare off your fish by getting too close, and you can damage your kayak. So, you want to judge your currents or drift well or, at least, react quickly. It helps when your kayak responds well to your maneuvering effort. You want to have your fishing pole in your hand most of the time and not your paddle. You want your lure to be in the highest probability strike zone for the maximum amount of time possible. That objective will lead to more fish on your line. You want a kayak that responds quickly and efficiently to your efforts to position it.

Sometimes your targets are the actual fish rather than the places they hang out. Very few fishing experiences equal the excitement of approaching fish that have already been sighted. Many fishermen specialize in *sightfishing*. While sightfishing, you do little casting until a fish is actually spotted. The oppurtunities may present themselves as: tailing redfish, bonefish, sheepshead (which all tail regularly), or bonnethead sharks which do not actually tail but roam the very shallow saltwater flats with their tail and dorsal fin showing. Even oddball species, such as carp, in freshwater and often in salt marshes present tail fishing oppurtunities. Largemouth bass at times present tailing oppurtunities during their spawning ritual. With the exception of the bass, the other species present intermittent targets as they feed on the bottom. When their heads go down to munch, their tails come up for a short time. Then, they disappear and reappear somewhere else. It is not always possible to tell if it is the same fish, or if there are a number of fish in the area. You never know how long a tail will be up, which side of the kayak your next oppurtunity will rise, or how far away. Bonnethead sharks on shallow saltwater flats are particularly challenging targets since they are in perpetual motion, and they are usually going at a pretty good clip. They can be obvious and alluring at one moment and vanish the next. They may reappear next to you or further away. Maneuverable kayaks are up to any of these challenges because they can quickly and quietly penetrate these shallow areas without spooking the fish and alter course, switching between oppurtunities very efficiently.

Often fish on the flats will not visibly show their fins; instead, they will leave a visible wake when moving. Even in deeper water, you will often see what is commonly called *nervous water* that betrays a school of fish near the surface over deeper water. This condition often appears as a patch of water that, more or less, looks different from the surrounding water surface. It can be a couple of feet, to more than twenty, even thirty feet or more across, depending upon the size and number of fish in a school. Sometimes the fins will stick out of the water. Perception of these subsurface schools, nervous waters and fins etc. are exaggerated for a kayaker, making them easier to see. The advantages that are lost from not spotting the actual fish are more than made up for by the advantages to spotting subsurface fish that leave these unmistakable clues. Needless to say, you want a fast kayak to get you into range and a maneuverable model to alter course quickly as the fish often change course unpredictably. Also, you want to avoid stumbling into a school of fish in shallow water.

Schooling fish in deeper water can pop up on the surface and begin busting baitfish very viciously. It commonly lasts from a couple seconds to a couple minutes. It can happen repeatedly sometimes for hours at a time. It happens in fresh and saltwater. When multiple schools are repeatedly popping up, you can bounce back and forth between schools for some of the most continous wild action that you will ever experience. A kayak that can accelerate quickly and change directions easily can be extremely efficient in this type of situation. The first time I got into one of these oppurtunities with my first kayak, I was extremely delighted at my Ocean Kayak *Scrambler XT's* performance. It was faster and more efficient than my 70 lb. thrust trolling motor on my flats boat. The kayak was quicker to turn, quicker to accelerate, even higher top speed for short distances and came to a stop quicker. It was high performance on schooling fish.

One of the most important advantages of some kayaks, to active casters, is the ability to leave the paddle lying *at-the-ready* on your lap. Sit-on-tops in general allow this practice, and sit-on-bottoms generally do not. Some sit-on-top anglers prefer to use a paddle holder in spite of the advantages of having a paddle ready on their lap to make small adjustments to positioning instantly with the use of one hand while the other hand holds the rod. They either do not mind picking up the paddle and replacing it in the holder each time they need it, do not need to make that many adjustments to their positioning for their style of fishing, haven't thought that much about it, haven't developed the skill of efficiently utilizing the paddle in this fashion, or are concerned about losing the paddle overboard. The last concern can be eliminated quickly by utilizing a paddle leash and by carrying an extra paddle. If you are an active kayak fisherman who is constantly casting, moving, searching, changing directions, adjusting position, and especially if you often hook strong fish around hang-ups and obstructions, then the ability and habit of keeping the paddle on your lap can add tremendously to your fishing efficiency and success.

Whether casting to oppurtunistic structure or cover situations along a bank or directly to fishy targets, you want your fishing rod in your hand most of the time instead of your paddle. The more time your offering spends in the proximity of the fish, the better your chances are of actually catching one. Therefor you want a kayak that responds well to your maneuvering efforts.

Wade-ability

Let's face it. Some people do not like to get out of a boat, fearing getting wet, drowning, sinking in mud, or various creature encounter fears. Others do not even want to buy a boat, preferring to wade fish. Fears aside, wading has many tactical advantages as well as economical advantages. For a wading angler, the kayak can drastically increase his potential and his safety factor for a small sacrifice financially. To the kayaker, wading can make some fishing situations even more efficient and can add to the comfort and enjoyment during a day's outing. It is an option with various advantages (see Chapter 9: *Kayakfishing Skills & Techniques*). Some kayaks are easier to climb into and out of than others. Shallow water, obviously, is easier than deeper water. Generally, sit-on-tops are easier than sit-on-bottoms. Some sit-on-tops are actually designed to be boarded successfully in water over the kayaker's head. These kayaks were designed for divers to climb overboard while anchored in deep water and to reboard after returning to the surface and removing dive gear. They even have a molded in depression at the rear of the kayak for placing dive tanks and strapping them in. Needless to say, these are wider and more stabile kayak designs, and they should be considered by any kayakfisherman who might be interested in adding wadefishing to his kayakfishing menu. All shallow water kayakfishermen should explore the possibilty and potential of kayak wadefishing.

Storage capacity

The limitation of storage space in a kayak is probably an actual advantage in a number of ways to kayak fishermen, but at the same time, we strive to maximize it. Because space is so limited, we carry less lures and tackle and become more selective. More thought goes into the process. Therefor, we make better choices and become more efficient and effective fishermen. We also spend less money and less time on maintenance and preparation. We are much more often ready to fish and tend to fish more often. But, we must have what we need for our particular fishing situations in order to increase our potential and versatility. Since, in most kayaks, the fisherman is in a more or less immobile position, accessibility becomes a major consideration when planning storage. If you can't reach it, you can't use it. Once again, stability comes into play here as some models of kayaks allow a kayaker to sit up with legs over the side in a *side saddle position*.This position allows a kayaker to access more of the storage areas than would otherwise be possible. Of course, if there is shallow water nearby, the kayaker can paddle inshore to access what is needed. However, in situations where there is no shallow water nearby or when you need immediate access to an item to capitalize on an oppurtunity, access is everything. When you consider kayak models for fishing, you should consider every item that you might need in the course of fishing in the probable situations you might encounter, and where it would best be placed to access it. The items you would need to access most often should be the most conveniently available. Keep versatility, options, and priorities in mind because you never know when you may discover a new favorite fish or new fishing hole, but you do not want to limit yourself in your most probable fishy endeavors. Make sure you consider add-on storage such as the possible addition of coolers, tackle bags, and also, heavily pocketed fishing shirts and vests. Even your hat should be considered. Consider where every item you might need would be placed, and how you might best access it.

Fish-ability

In addition to the previously mentioned considerations of paddle-ability, maneuverability, stability, wade-ability, and storage capacity which all add to the fish-ability of a kayak, there are also some other considerable *fish-ability factors* including attachability of items such as sea anchors, anchors, nets, rods, rod holders, paddle holders, and coolers. Does the outer structure of the kayak you are considering allow for the attachment of required accessories? Fish fighting dynamics should also be considered. Longer kayaks will prevent you from fighting your fish 360 degrees around the kayak at close quarters. You may have to fight the fish from the wrong side of the kayak, bending your rod under the keel. It is less efficient and even less enjoyable. With a shorter kayak, you can follow the fish more efficiently, control the battle and see what is actually happening. Without the use of a paddle, you can actually turn your kayak broadside to the fish, creating more resistance to the fish, or you can point the bow directly toward the fish and allow him to tow you around. In some cases, you can poke or prod a fish with rod jabs to strategically change his direction and then follow him as he heads into more favorable waters to do battle away from obstructions, other boats, et cetera. A shorter more maneuverable kayak makes this tactic easier to accomplish.

Once successful at battling a fish into submission, a new challenge often presents itself to the kayaker to varying degrees, depending upon which species of fish you have hooked into and how large. Different species of fish present their own peculiar challenges (see the chapters on *Kayak Fish Handling & Kayakfishing Safety*). Ladyfish, even after a long fight, tend to jump a great deal. A low-on-the-water kayaker makes a high probability target for a treble hooked plug attached to these high flyers. Large, high jumping fish such as tarpon might become an unwelcome inhabitant of your kayak. Some fish, such as cobia often fight harder after being boated. They are large and powerful fish that can do a lot of damage even in conventional boats not prepared to deal with them. Should you be fortunate enough to battle and even subdue such an adversary, and if you are planning to keep and eat it, you will need a plan and epquipment such as a net, gaff, fish club, pliers and storage suitable to prevent spoilage. Some kayakers store their big fish below the outer deck on a sit-on-top kayak. They access this valuable storage space via a hatch which usually has a waterproof hatch cover. If you plan to do any livebait fishing, then you will need to work out a plan for keeping your live bait alive (see Chapter 12: *Kayak Live Bait Fishing*).

Transportability

You will need to transport your kayak from your storage area in your garage etc. to your vehicle and from your vehicle to the water and back again. On the water, you may need to portage around rapids or other impedimentary situations on a river or from one body of water to another, depending on the environment you choose to fish. Shorter, lighter kayaks are easier to handle in such situations. Small boat trailers can be used with kayaks to avoid lifting larger kayaks onto cartop situations, but for the most part, kayaks are usually cartopped. Shorter kayaks can be slid into the back of pickup trucks or vans in an upright position. They can be rigged and loaded with all your gear at-the-ready so you can save time when you leave home, launch at the lake or load up to go home. This condition of readiness and convenience can lead to more fishing trips since you will always be ready and require less time to prepare, go, and return home. If you have a pickup truck or van and have a place to store your kayak fully rigged and ready to fish, then consider a kayak size that might be transported in this manner. A little nine footer might be great for pond hopping or other short paddling situations, and it will fit into the back of your overland transportation more conveniently. A twelve footer, however, might be more useful where you intend to fish if you expect a longer paddle. A fifteen footer would be impractical and awkward to use in this manner. Once again you must calculate the tradeoffs.

Affordability

The most affordable kayak is the one you already own. If you already have a kayak and want to take up kayakfishing, you do not need to buy a new kayak just for fishing. You may choose to do that later, but it would be advisable to try your present kayak first. Consider whether it can be customized to enhance its usefulness for your fishing pursuits (see Chapter 6: *Customize Your Kayak*). Test it and see how it stacks up, according to the guidelines outlined in this chapter. Even if you find that you do want to purchase another kayak for fishing, wait until you are sure what you need and make the best choice. If you are having trouble fishing from it or if you seem to be struggling, consider whether a little customizing might help, or perhaps, you actually need to go shopping for a more fisher-friendly model. But first, get some on the water experience so you will know what to look for in your next kayak.

When kayak shopping, look for the plastic polyethylene models. They come in both sit-on-top and sit-on-bottom models. They are very economical: roughly about $500, depending on the model, and they are very durable. Sit-on-tops are usually plastic, but sit-on-bottoms can often be fibreglass or kevlar. Fibreglass and kevlar are usually more expensive than plastic kayaks, but the techniques used in their construction allow for superior designs. Of course, superior designs yield superior performance, but the plastic kayaks do yield great performance, and the mass manufacturing techniques allow for a much more affordable price.

The best deal that you can probably get would be to purchase someone else's used kayak. They are not easy to find, especially in the exact model that you may want. Try checking at kayak rental businesses. Even if they do not have a used kayak available try checking in with them on a regular basis. You can get a list of dealers in your area from the manufacturer. Many of the dealers are also rental outlets. Rental outlets often replace their kayaks and canoes seasonally. They often sell off their old kayaks and buy all new kayaks at the same time because they get a better deal when they buy in volume. Timing is the key. Ask the manager when he anticipates buying new kayaks. Ask if he will call you when some used models become available. Check back in with him regularly just in case he forgets. The deal can be worth it.

My first kayak was a used rental Ocean Kayak *Scrambler XT*. I rented it for a day to test my theory that it might be worth fishing from it. When I climbed onboard at the lake, I had second thoughts. The perspective was so low that I felt as if I were sinking. After a few minutes however, I made the mental adjustment. The perspective from so low on the water was remindful of my tubefloat days, but the mobility was swift and stealthy. I knew it was a winner even before a 4-1/2 pound largemouth bass leaped out of the lily pads and pounced on my lure. I couldn't wait to get back to the dealer and ask what he would charge me to keep the whole setup. He sent me out with the *Scrambler XT*, paddles, Summit high back rest, paddles, paddle leash, bowline, anchor, and foam cartop carriers. For $600, I drove the whole deal home.

Comfort

How important is your comfort while in your kayak? How

long do you plan to spend in your kayak? Discomfort can really distract you when you are trying to fish, and it detracts immensely from enjoyment of the experience. Many of us are willing to suffer a little under adverse circumstances in order to experience outstanding fishing. Hot sunshine, freezing rain, hail and blood-thirsty mosquitoes all get their licks in, but a wise kayakfisherman starts with the most comfortable kayak he can find. One of the most important factors is the backrest. You want a high backrest with as much support as you can get. Sit-on-top kayaks give you the option of buying the backrest of your choice. Choose a high-backed model with a large pocket in back (see Chapter 6: *Customizing Your Kayak* & Chapter 7: *Kayakfishing Accessories*). If you also choose a kayak model that allows cooler storage just behind the seat, then you can lean your high backrest back against the cooler for additional support. Also, you can stuff the back pocket on the backrest with raingear and sweathirts to create a soft pillow against the cooler, and you will be comfortable enough to fall asleep in your kayak. Be careful, however, because you may wake up in another state.

Sitting side saddle on a *Scrambler XT*

One of the problems with sit on bottom kayaks often heard from kayakers is that your legs are trapped inside the kayak. Changes of position are very limited. With the more stable designs of sit-on-tops, the kayaker can change to many positions to get relief. You can even sit sideways and fish with your legs hanging over the sides almost like sitting on the end of a dock. In addition, sit-on-tops are easy to slip in and out of which makes it easier to slip overboard in shallow water to stand for awhile or wade fish which is a nice relaxing break at times.

Some anglers that fish colder and deeper waters have no interest in getting out of the kayak to wade and even less interest in getting wet. They prefer to stay dry and warm. Sit-on-bottom kayaks are preferred in the norteastern U.S., and they are often used in combination with a spray skirt to keep water out of the kayak. Sit-on-top kayaks are self bailing, which means that water that enters the kayak over the gunnels or from rain, will exit the kayak via *scupper holes* in the bottom of the kayak. However, small amounts of water also enter the kayak through these holes. *Scupper hole plug*s are available to prevent water from entering via these drain holes, but if a wave comes over the side, the water will be unable to run out with the plugs in place. The scupper plugs work well while fishing calm waters. In warm weather and especially on hot summer days, most sit-on-top kayakers appreciate the cooling effects of letting a little water drain through the kayak and even enjoy getting at least a little wet. In colder weather, wetsuits will keep you warm, and neoprene waders with a rainjacket will keep you warm and dry.

Test or tryout

Before buying a kayak, you should consider renting the same model first to be sure your money is well spent. Tell the dealer you intend to buy a kayak as soon as you can identify the model that is right for you. Ask if he has a *try out* policy. Perhaps he has a used model around that you can test. If not, ask if he would be willing to *discount the rental fee* from the purchase price if you decide to buy the kayak. If you are unfamiliar with kayaks, you may even want to take a kayaking lesson or, even better yet, take a guided trip with a professional kayakfishing guide. Not only will you get to try out his kayak choice, but you will also get to see how he has customized his kayak. Of course, you will also get to learn some invaluable fishing secrets, including some places to fish. Unfortunately, there are very few professional kayakfishing guides available. There is a list of kayakfishing guides in Chapter 16: *Kayakfishing Experts* and also in Chapter 17: *Kayakfishing Resources*. If there are no kayakfishing guides in your area, you might try taking a kayak float trip with a professional outfitter. If so, try to get to use a kayak style that you are considering to buy. Another and cheaper alternative would be to hook up with an experienced kayakfisherman who can share his hard earned experience with you. Most kayakfishermen are excited to meet other kayakfishermen and potential kayakfishermen. Most seem eager to share and transfer their experience to others. You might be able to meet a few by inquiring around paddle and fishing tackle shops. The Internet chat and bulletin boards may be your best chance of finding someone in your area to hookup with. If you are unable to meet with someone in person, then you will at least get to read histories of conversation on the bulletin boards and perhaps start up a rewardful conversation. There are a number of fishing websites that have bulletin boards where fishermen leave messages in the form of questions or advice posted (see Chapter 3: *Kayakfishing Community and Communications*).

Sit-On-Top or Sit-On-Bottom

So, the question often arises. Sit-on-top or sit-on-bottom? Which is better? Well, that is a question with multiple answers that only you can choose. If you live in a cooler climate, do not like the idea of getting wet, and do not want to wear neoprene waders, wetsuits, rainjackets etc. in cooler weather or seasons, then you might be happier in a sit-on-bottom kayak. However, if you like getting a little wet, or you do not mind wearing neoprene waders, wetsuits, rainjackets etc. in cooler weather, if you need to get into and out of your kayak to dive or wade, if you need a larger cargo capacity, and if you need the advantages of leaving a paddle at-the-ready on your lap to respond quickly to oppurtunities rather than retrieving and placing the paddle into a paddleholder, then a sit-on-top kayak is probably your best choice. Now let me see, which make and model sit-on-top (or sit-on-bottom) kayak should I buy?

Kayak Model Recommendations

So, which models do professionals, experts and experienced kayakfishermen recommend? Well, it seems predictably to vary according to paddling environments, fishing requirements and personal choice. However, a survey of kayak anglers will usually yield the same model preferences repeatedly from the myriad of kayak models manufactured. Dennis Spike of Coastal Kayak Fishing probably said it best that—*there are probably about ten models of sit-on-tops on the market that are truly fishable.* He has probably fished more models than most of us, and he says that he is still searching for his favorite model.

By contrast, John Stanton knows exactly what he wants, and he has found it in the *Tribalance Kayak.* John is an east coast Florida kayakfishing flats guide who specializes in sightfishing for redfish. He wants the ability to easily stand in his kayak, giving him the advantage of height to spot his quarry. Capt. Butch Rickey is a west coast Florida flatsguide who started out in the wrong kayak and found that he did not like getting his butt wet. In addition, he also found that he needed a bigger kayak to accomadate his larger size in order to stay dry. He is now happily paddling a Perception *Swing.* Ken Sigvardson also likes to stay dry because he fishes cold northeastern waters and recommends two sit-on-bottom models. Ken's favorite model is the *Pachena* by Current Designs, but he usually recommends the *Acadia* by Perception Kayaks to beginners because it is cheaper, wider, and more initially stabile. Mark Ambrozic from Ontario, Canada is the designer of the the First Mate which is a rod, paddle, tackle holder and trolling system for sit-on-bottom kayaks. Obviously, he prefers sit-on-bottom kayaks. Mark likes the Paluski *Spirit* because it is inexpensive, durable, lightweight, comfortable, and handles well. Rick Roberts is the southeastern representative for Heritage Kayaks, and he prefers a sit-on-top kayak, but similar to Capt. Butch Rickey, he likes to keep his butt dry. So, he prefers the higher riding Heritage Kayaks. He especially likes the paddling efficiency of their superior designs. His favorite models are the *Expedition* and the *Osprey*. Jackson Reade agrees with Rick on the Heritage design since he requires the paddling efficiency in his efforts to keep up with what is happening as much as is possible on the flats of the Banana River *No-Motor-Zone* in Florida where he is a guide for kayak saltwater flatsfishermen. Jackson likes the Heritage *Shearwater* which may be one of the fastest kayaks on the water.

Some models are recommended repeatedly by many experts and experienced kayak anglers. Ocean Kayak's *Scupper Pro* model is one of the most frequently mentioned, especially by big water paddlers. Jim Sammons of La Jolla Kayak Fishing in California prefers the *Scupper Pro TW* which is the model with a tankwell that allows you to place a cooler behind the seat and strap it in. The cooler can serve as storage for your gear or your catch and function as a live bait tank. He says that they are fast and durable. George Whillock, who fishes off the Gulf Coast of Alabama for big game fish with live bait, also uses the *Scupper Pro*. Tommy Stubblefield, an experienced kayakfisherman and expert fishing kayak rigger from the Texas coast, also prefers the model. Vivian Oliva, who fishes the southwestern Florida coast, paddles a *Scupper Pro* but prefers the model with a center hatch and twin hatches fore and aft because she likes to take overnight trips and needs the extra room for camping gear. Vivian also likes the model's stability, speed, and seaworthiness, and she especially likes the service she gets from the people at Ocean Kayak. The *Scrambler XT* is another model of Ocean Kayak that has won the respect of many experienced kayakfishermen like David Sims of Action Watersports in Auburndale, Florida. David sells many makes and models of kayaks both wholesale and retail, but he prefers the *Scrambler XT* to customize and rig for fishing due to its durability, economy, intermediate size, handling characteristics, versatility, and stability.

The Aquaterra/Perception *Prism* is another model that is popular and frequently mentioned on message boards on the Internet.

Texas saltwater flats kayakfishing guide Capt. Allen Cartmell uses four of them that he carries onboard his flatsboat until he reaches his selected fishing areas. Matt Fuller, a very active Texas kayakfisherman, uses the model in both fresh and saltwater. Florida kayakfishing guide Jackson Reade uses several Aquaterra *Prisms* that he has rigged with five gallon buckets as aerated live bait tanks. There are other commonly mentioned kayaks that are used for kayakfishing such as the Cobra *Fisherman* which kayak flyfishing guide Gary Bulla uses in southern California and Baja waters. Texas kayakfisherman and retired Florida Keys fishing guide Barry Evans chose the Wilderness Systems' *Ride* after doing some extensive research before making his choice. The model is another that is often recommended on the message boards of the Internet. Regardless of recommendations, all professionals, experts and experienced kayakfishermen agree that you should— *try before you buy.*

Chapter Six

Customize Your Kayak

Jackson Reade's customized *Prism*

If you have an old kayak laying around, you probably do not need to buy a new kayak to kayakfish, and even if you do buy a new kayak, there are a few things you can do to make it or an old kayak more *fisher-friendly*. There are many different kayak models, fishing situations, fishing objectives and styles of fishing. Still, there are some needs that most kayakfishermen have in common. Some of the most important aspects of a *fisher-friendly* kayak are a good comfortable backrest, rodholders, a paddle leash, paddle holder/clip, an anchor, a cooler, and ample storage. The challenge in customizing your kayak is in figuring out where to put everything in a manner that the items you need are *at-the-ready*. The items you need most and most often should be convenient to reach and use while on the water. Each different kayak design has its own limitations and challenges to making it into your personal ultimate fishing craft. First, you will have to locate potential attachment sites for all of those common necessities. Then identify potential storage areas for all of the fishing tackle, gear and other things that you may need to take with you, especially those items that are required by the style of fishing you plan to do. Having or not having an item with you can make all the difference in fishing comfort, fishing longevity, fishing enjoyment, fishing success, or even fishing safety. All fishing trips are not created equal, and some endeavors require more planning and preparedness. Needless to say, kayakfishermen need to travel light, but at the same time, it pays to plan for versatility and maximum storage.

Backrests

You should get the best backrest that you can find for your kayak. An aching back makes it very difficult to concentrate on fishing; much less enjoy it. Back pain can chase you home early, and you cannot catch fish there. One of the best style backrests for sit-on-top kayaks is a high backed thermomolded model. It has a high back with a large storage pouch on the back (see photo on page 95). Surf to Summit manufactures this style of backrest that are sold in many paddle shops across the country. Ocean Kayak and Surf to Summit have this style backrest featured on their websites. Some sit-on-top kayaks have an area just behind the seat that is molded to receive a cooler and hold it in place. When you stuff the back pouch on the backrest with raingear or sweatshirts, it makes an excellent pillow to lean back against the cooler. Some sit on bottom kayaks, especially some fibreglass models, have backrests molded into the kayak.

Backrest Rodholders

A new model of backrest coming out from Surf to Summit will be of special interest to kayakfishermen. It has two rodholders built into the back panel. The rodholders are holster style with PVC inserts and are reportedly sturdy enough to use while trolling. At the time of this writing it is not yet available, but it should be on the market very soon.

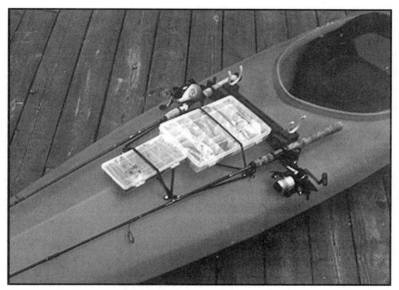

The *First Mate* from I.I. Endeavors also holds your paddle

Rodholders/Paddle holders

You can fish out of a kayak without rodholders, but they sure are a convenience. Even though you can have a rod or two laying between your legs, the option of rodholders, the convenience and the advantages of rodholders insist on their installation. You have many choices of style, function and installation. If you plan to do any live bait fishing or trolling, then they are almost a necessity. Some merely hold extra backup rods in the event that you might need them at some point in your day. Others actually keep a variety of rods with varying applications at-the-ready to capitalize on fast changing oppurtunities. Different rods can be available for various line sizes, artificial lure types, or even different target species as oppurtunities present themselves during your outing. Some rodholders are actually incorporated into a paddle holder and store your rods as well as your paddle while not in use, or they can secure your rods for rough situations such as surf launching. At least one rod/paddle holder combo secures a rod while actively fishing in a trolling position. The best answer for your particular setup may be a combination of rodholder types. You do not want to carry too many rods out in a disorderly clump. Murphy's Law will have a field day. Fortunately there are a number of options.

One of the best rod holders is the flush mounted rodholder (see photo on page 81). It is one of the more involved installations, requiring a larger cutout hole, but it is one of the most convenient and useful rodholders. It is effective as a secure rodholder for trolling or live bait fishing, and it works great for storing a number of rods at-the-ready. In addition, a rodholder of this type placed behind your seat can also hold an umbrella there to give yourself relief from the sun when you need it. If you have a model of kayak that is *stackable* one on top of the other, this type of rodholder will not interfere with snug stacking. The stacking ability of some models of sit-on-top kayaks is very helpful when storing kayaks or transporting multiple kayaks on a single cartop carrier or on a larger boat. This type of rodholder can instantly be converted to an above the deck raised rodholder of any height by inserting a section of PVC pipe with a matching diameter. Flush mounted rodholders come in three screw hole and two screw hole models. These rodholders are designed for conventional boats, but they work fine on kayaks although you may have to cut them down in length to fit inside the hull. The bottom end of the tube needs to be closed off with epoxy clay so that water will not enter your hull (see Installing a Flush Mounted Rodholder later in this chapter). Use blind rivets to fasten them to the hull. Three screw hole rodholders have a wider phlange and can be used where you have enough space. Two screw hole rodholders can be used in more narrow areas, but the narrow phlange calls for an accurate installation.

Flushmounted rodholder

When mounting rodholders at the forward end of your kayak, consider that the rods placed there will be in your way if you intend to cast ahead of your kayak. You may not need to install many rodholders there. Also, they should be installed just beyond your paddle reach so as not to impede your normal stroke range. However, they should not be out of your reach when you need your rod quickly. When installing flushmount rodholders, consider the angle of your hull on your forward deck or gunnels. Your upright rod will lean according to that contour. The forward rodholder is great for keeping one rod at-the-ready while you are paddling. It usually does not matter which way a forward mounted rod at-the-ready leans, but a leaning rod will help keep a dangling lure from hanging up on the rod. It is also a great location for a trolling rod, but a trolling rodholder should lean outward as much as possible. For mounting rods on the forward deck of a sit-on-top kayak that are fully adjustable to lean according to your changing needs, consider installing a RHYNOBAR and attaching adjustable rail mount rodholders (see Chapter 7: *Kayakfishing Accessories*). Many rail mount models are adjustable in any direction.

Crossed rods lean inward

You can also troll from the rear of the kayak. Trolling from the rear of the kayak gives you the advantage of having the bow of the kayak clear for casting lures out the front with a second rod as you travel forward. The rear trolling rod also leans outward though, and you must avoid inadvertantly reaching back and hanging up on it while casting. While the outward leaning, rear trolling rodholder is great for trolling, it is not the best angle for a rod stored at-the-ready. It creates an unecessary casting hazard. Actually, at-the-ready rodholders stored at the rear behind your seat should be upright or lean slightly inward to keep the tips of the rods from extending out over the water and in harms way of your backcast. Two rods mounted on either side of the kayak behind the seat might cross each other in the middle of the kayak (see photo on page 82). If you install flush-mounted rodholders, you can also utilize them as raised tube rodholders by simply inserting a section of an appropriate diameter of PVC pipe of the desired height into the rodholder. Unfortunately, kayaks are not generally designed for kayakfishing, and even less

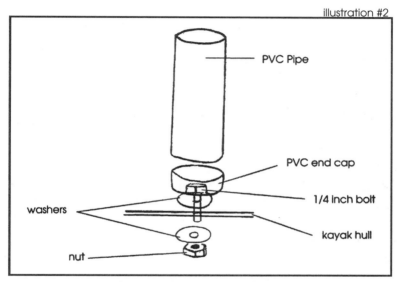

illustration #2

PVC Pipe

PVC end cap

1/4 inch bolt

washers

kayak hull

nut

Homemade PVC rodholder

for versatile kayakfishing. Not all designs will allow you to customize to perfection. So, it pays to keep these concepts in mind when buying or customizing a kayak. Compromise is often necessary, but creativity can make up for much of what is lacking in design. A really well designed or customized kayak can be a versatile and efficient fishing platform.

Another style of rodholder to consider is very popular on the west coast in California. It requires only a small hole drilled into the hull of the kayak. A stainless steel bolt passes through the hull with a large washer on either side of the hull. The bolt fastens into a PVC end cap with the open end facing up. The outer washer and a nut fasten it snugly to the kayak hull. A longer PVC tube inserts into the end cap. The rod handle, of course, goes into the tube. One of the neat things about this upright rodholder is that the longer tube can be removed when the rodholder is not in use, leaving only the end cap. Handling and transporting the kayak is much easier without the rodholders protruding. This style of rodholder is especially useful for placing rodholders in difficult areas where flushmounted rodholders will not work. You can make one of these nifty rodholders yourself or you can buy one ready made from Dennis Spike at Coastal Kayak Fishing in Reseda, California.

One of the most ingenious rodholder/paddle holder combinations on the kayakfishing scene is the invention of Mark Ambrozic of I.I. Endeavors in Toronto, Ontario. This patented invention is designed for sit-on-bottom kayaks. It is designed for fast, easy installation and is not permanent. It requires no holes or alterations to your kayak. The First Mate, as it is called, holds one or two rods securely and will allow you to place one rod in trolling position. It will also hold your paddle, and shock cords hold your tackle boxes in place on the deck in front of you (see photo on page 79). The First Mate will fit many models of sit-on-bottom kayaks. The FirstMate is great for travelers using rental kayaks since it can be attached quickly without altering the kayak, and it fits so many models of sit-on-bottom kayaks. To determine which models and to see additional photos of the First Mate, write to them for their brochure or visit their website at http://webhome.idirect.com/~aboo/.

Plastic ice chests or coolers can be used to add rodholders to your kayak. If your kayak is designed to accept an ice chest or cooler into a molded-in receptacle type area, typically behind the seat, then you can attach standard rodholders to the cooler. If your kayak has good straps to hold the cooler in place, then the rodholders can be used to troll or use live bait. In the event of a large fish striking, they will be solid enough to prevent the loss of your rod or even the cooler. Of course, they would also be adequate for storage of rods at-the-ready, but perhaps not quite so ready as rods closer at hand in other styles of rodholders in a more convenient location. Properly setup, a kayak angler could easily have a dozen rods within reasonable access.

A rod holding product called Rodsaver can also be used to store rods, paddles or other gear on the lid of the cooler. It is a heavy velcro folding strap that usually holds rods in place on the deck of a conventional boat. It can also be used on the fore or aft deck of sit-on-bottom kayaks or on the gunnels of sit-on-top kayaks. It also makes a very nifty paddle holder.

Another style of cooler makes a great storage device right off the store shelf. The Igloo Softmate 48 can cooler fits perfectly into the cooler well on some models of Ocean Kayaks. It has a soft but durable outer cover with a hard plastic shell inside. The

Igloo Softmate holding a spare rod

outer cover has a mesh side pouch that will accept the butts of several spinning rods, and a double set of straps with velcro that can be used to hold the rod shafts. The rod shafts can be held even more securely in place by the kayak's strap that goes over the top to secure the cooler to the kayak. Several rods can be secured to the top of the cooler lid by the straps, and also, by wrapping the velcro enclosed handles around the shaft. The cooler interior can carry your wallet, keys, camera, tackle, lunch, drinks, and perhaps even your catch if you choose. One of the advantages of this particular cooler is that you do not need to unzip or fully open the lid to place items into or out of the cooler. Simply unzipping one end and bending the lid upward is sufficient to place a sizeable fish headfirst into the cooler, conserving the cool air inside.

Coolers can be a great way to add rodholders and other storage convenience to your kayak and to borrowed or rental kayaks when you are away from home, or perhaps, for those who do not yet own a kayak. If you know the model of kayak you are able to rent in another state while on vacation, you can travel lite and be confident that you will have the gear needed onboard for an enjoyable and successful trip. Kayakfishermen, away on business trips, can also capitalize on great fishing oppurtinities that would otherwise be too much of a hassle with a limited amount of time available.

Storage

While on the subject of coolers and storage, consider that a cooler is probably the best place to store your live bait, and they are commonly used as a live bait tank by serious live bait fishermen. There are four reasons: it has adequate volume; it is insulated to help keep bait cool; it can be aerated to keep oxygen sensitive and fragile bait alive for long periods of time, and it allows you to transport bait over land to your fishing location. Either airstone aerators or recirculation agitating aerators can be used (see Chapter 12: *Kayak Live Bait Fishing*). The drawback is that the use of an aerator requires the use of a battery. Some aerators are designed to use small flashlite batteries, and some require large 12 volt batteries. However, you can go to a battery specialty store and choose from a variety of compact size 12 volt batteries that will get the job done without undue weight in your kayak. If you want to avoid the hassles of the batteries altogether and eliminate the noise factor, check out a product called The

Oxygen Edge from Oxygenation Systems of Texas. Their system delivers pure oxygen to your baitwell water straight from a storage tank (see Chapter 12: *Kayak Live Bait Fishing* and Chapter 17: *Kayakfishing Resources*).

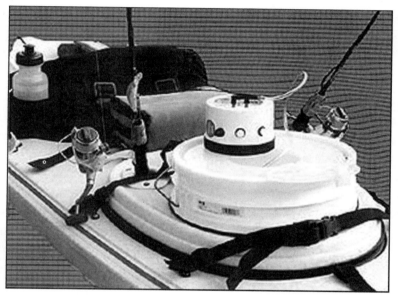

Jackson Reade's custom hatch bucket live bait tank

There are other alternatives for storing live bait that do not require you to give up your valuable cooler space. Florida kayak flatsfishing guide Jackson Reade designed a live bait tank where a five gallon bucket is fitted into a hatch cover (see photo above). He uses a a battery operated airstone aerator to add oxygen to the water. Live baitfish that you catch on the water can be placed in a trolling bucket. While fishing or light paddling, the bucket can be left overboard. When you want to paddle more swiftly, however, you can lift it into the kayak for short periods as it will retain about half the volume of water. Periodically, it should be set back overboard to exchange the water for freshly oxygenated water. Some anglers simply lay baitfish in the flooded footwells of self bailing sit-on-top kayaks. The constant interchange of fresh water helps to keep them alive. It works very well in situations where the baitfish are relatively easy to catch and can be used and replaced rather easily. Crabs that are too large to exit through the scupper holes can also be kept alive indefinitely in the flooded footwells, but you would want to remove the pincers with a pair of pliers. Clams which are relatively easy to catch while in your kayak can be fantastic bait for many species of fish and can be kept alive very easily in your flooded footwell or your cooler. Live shrimp can easily escape through the scupper holes unless you place them in a mesh bag. Live shrimp can also be kept alive in your cooler in an open plastic bag if you are careful not to place them directly on the ice.

If you plan your kayak for maximum storage capacity, giving up your cooler space for live bait need not be a problem. Many models of kayaks provide one or more hatches which allow access to the interior of the kayak hull. These roomy storage areas can swallow up a lot of gear. Bulkier items such as camping gear and cast nets can be stored there. Some hatches on some models of kayaks are not readily accessible while afloat. So, plan *what you put where* according to when you will need it. Hatches are not always entirely water tight. If you have items that are important to keep dry, then you should place them in dry storage bags (see *Chapter 17: Kayakfishing Acessories*) before placing them inside the hatch. These heavy duty plastic bags are easy to use, work very well, and come in a variety of sizes. They work great for cameras, GPS units and cell phones. Deck netting is a pattern of elastic cords that serve to trap items placed under it in place. It is very useful for tackle boxes or anything you want to be easily accessible but want to prevent from falling overboard. Deck netting can turn open areas of the deck into useful storage areas. Since deck netting is usually used in open areas, tackleboxes or other items stored under it need watertight containers or dry storage bags, unless getting wet is not a problem. Even the use of such items as large pocketed fishing shirts, fishing vests, and even fishing hats can help to add storage and carry a few extra items that may be useful to your trip. Although kayakers should strive to travel lite, there is a long list of accessories and epquipment that might be helpful or needed on your trip. So, it pays to maximize your storage potential on your kayak.

Anchor

An anchor is one of those things that you just don't want to leave home without. There are many days and many situations where you will not use your anchor one time all day. However, an anchor is one of those items that—when you need it—you really need it bad. It can sometimes change a windy unfishable day into a bonanza if you know how to use it (see Chapter 9: *Kayakfishing Skills & Techniques*). A standard folding kayak anchor is a must, but you should install a quick change clip in order to change to specialty anchors when the situation calls for it. Specialty anchors may simply be a heavier or lighter anchor or perhaps a chain. Use no more anchor rope than you need for your fishing destinations, and place your anchor attachment site on your kayak where you can easily reach it. Some kayakfishermen rig sophisticated movable anchoring systems with a carabiner which allows the anchor attachment position to change variably from the aft, midship, or the bow of the kayak. Such a system allows the ultimate in kayak positioning in respect to the effects of the current or wind.

Paddle leash

A paddle leash (see page 96) is extremely important to active fishermen who are on the move and repeatedly casting to various targets and need to constantly use the paddle to adjust position or move a little forward or backward. It works well with sit-on-tops. You do not have to continually put the paddle in and out of a paddle holder. The paddle stays in your lap where you can use it constantly (see Chapter 9: *Kayakfishing Skills & Techniques*). Even when fighting or gaffing a large fish (see photo on page 15). It is one of the greatest advantages of sit-on-top kayaks for fishing. The paddle may seem as if it could fall from your lap and may even slip a bit, but it will rarely fall off into the water altogether. With a paddle leash, it will not matter even if it does fall overboard (see Chapter 7: *Kayakfishing Accessories*).

Paddle holder

If you are not setting up a sit-on-top kayak, if you are not comfortable with a paddle in your lap or the possibility of it falling overboard even on a paddle leash, then you may want to install a paddle holder. A paddle holder is very convenient, and it can be used with a paddle leash. If your style of fishing doesn't require that you are constantly on the move, picking up and putting down the paddle, then you will probably appreciate a paddle holder. Bait and bottomfishermen often sit in one place for extended periods of time and a paddle holder can get a lot of appreciated use in such situations. As mentioned previously, many paddle holders double as rodholders. For kayakfishermen who launch in the surf, paddle/rodholders are often popular because the upright rodholders are not a safe place to keep rods while launching or returning in the surf where there is a threat of an overturn. The rods can then be brought down to the paddle/rodholders for more secure storage. However, when installing paddle holders, consider whether they will be in the way of your paddle stroke, especially when you are tired. When you are tired, your paddle stroke changes, and you tend not to clear the kayak or paddle holders at times. Also, if you have more than one kayak of the same model that has a *stacking capability* to store or transport them, check to see if the paddle holder installation will interfere with this convenience.

Eyelets

Eyelet attachment clips are great. You don't want to sit on them, but it seems that everywhere you put them: you find something you need to hook onto them.They are often installed by manufacturers to attach backrest straps. They are great for bunji cords to hold items in your kayak or to hold your kayak in your pickup truck. You can even use them to hold your kayak in a larger boat. You can install them with a rivet gun anywhere on your kayak to attach such items as anchor ropes, paddle leashes, trolling buckets, sea anchors, bowlines and more.

Eyelet

Straps & Fast Clipping Buckles

Some models of sit-on-top kayaks come from the manufacturer with nylon straps and fast clipping buckles installed. The rear of the backrests are often held in position by nylon staps. Molded-in cooler wells also come with one or more straps to hold a cooler in its position. Even the recessed front deck on some sit-on-tops have a strap that is very useful to hold such things as tackle bags or boxes in position. Straps and buckles are available in many hardware and fabric stores as well as some kayak dealers. They can be added anywhere on your kayak with a blind rivet and a large washer.

Repairing Your Kayak

Kayaks are durable and tough, but should you damage your kayak, you can easily make repairs. If you have a fibreglass kayak, you can repair it easily with one of many fibreglass repair kits on the market. They are available at most local marine stores. Plastic polyethylene kayaks are really tough and difficult to damage but easy to repair. Heat guns are available to patch any hole you are capable of inflicting on your kayak. Before spending for a heat gun, check with your local dealer. He may have one. It may be cheaper to have him make the repairs than to invest in the heat gun yourself, and the chances of you redamaging your kayak are probably slim. Ocean Kayak has an instructional video on making kayak repairs.

Cut-out and rivet holes

Installing a Flush Mount Rodholder

1. Buy standard flushmounted rodholder.
2. Remember, before installing, to consider and check where the rod will lean after inserting into rodholder.
3. Hold it upside down centered on the area you plan to install it and out line the wide phlange at the top.
4. You need a circular cut out saw for your drill that is the same diameter as the widest outer diameter of the tube in your rodholder.

5. Center the cutout saw on the area within your outline of the phlange.

6. After cutting out the hole, insert the rodholder tube into the kayak to check the depth available.

7. You probably will have to cut down the tube of the rodholder with a hacksaw. Standard rodholders are usually too long for most kayaks. Cut the rodholder tube to the longest length that will possibly insert into the kayak.

8. After inserting rodholder to where the phlange sits snug on the kayak hull, use a magic marker to mark the screw holes.

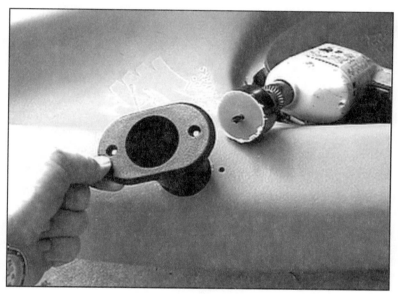

Insert rodholder

9. Check your drill bits and select a bit that matches the diameter of your rivets.

10. Drill out the holes, insert the rodholder and check that the screw holes match.

11. Since you don't want water to enter your kayak via rodholders, you will need to close off the bottom end with two part epoxy clay. Mix the epoxy.

12. Flatten like a pancake and press flat onto the bottom end of the rodholder. Let it cure.

13. After it cures, smother the bottom end in silicone.
14. Place silicone around the perimeter of the cutout.
15. Insert the rodholder.
16. Fasten the rodholder with rivets in the screwholes.
17. Allow the silicone to cure.

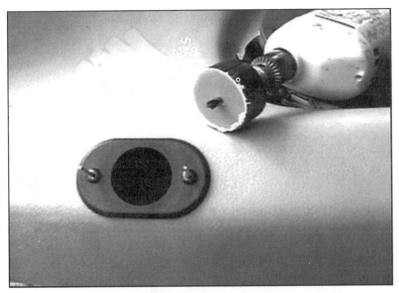

Rivets in screwholes

Chapter Seven

Kayakfishing Accessories

Customized accessories

It is the acccessories that make a kayak, fishable, comfortable, transportable, convenient, effective, efficient, versatile, and safe. It is also the accessories that turn a kayak into a fishing machine. The contact information for most of the items mentioned in this chapter can be found in Chapter 17: *Kayakfishing Resources*, including the phone numbers, addresses, websites and email addresses.

Paddles

There are many styles of paddles to choose from. Two piece models are much more convenient than a long single piece paddle. Expert kayakers will fuss over symetrical and asymetrical designs, paddling styles and efficiencies, and there is much to be learned from them as you gain experience at kayaking. But generally, lightweight paddles with moderate asymetrical blades are better for relaxed long distance paddling. Larger, wider blades are good for sprint paddling to reach breaking fish quickly or to avoid rocks with a power stroke when drifting downstream in river currents. For more information refer to the Kayaking Book List in Chapter 17: *Kayakfishing Resources*.

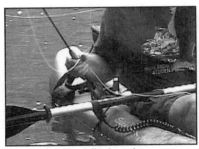
Paddle leash

Cooler as a backrest

Paddle leashes

With a paddle leash attached to your paddle, you will not have to worry about it falling overboard and drifting away when you are preoccupied with casting or fighting a fish. You can let it lay in your lap, put it in a paddle holder, or throw it overboard. It just doesn't matter. A paddle leash gives you great piece of mind about the paddle. It is a must. Find one with a quick connect attachment to the kayak and a velcro wrap around the paddle.

Backrests

A good backrest may be the most important accessory on your

kayak. In a kayak, comfort is everything. If your back is hurting, you will probably go home. If you are comfortable, you will stay, fish well, catch fish, and go again. Get the best backrest you can buy for your kayak. For sit-on-tops, you want to buy a high backed backrest of the thermo-molded type. If you can find one, get one with a large storage pocket on the back. If you have a kayak model that accepts a cooler behind the seat, you can stuff the back pocket with raingear and sweatshirts to create a fluffy pillow to lean back against your cooler. The extra storage potential is also always appreciated. As an added bonus, some companies include a distress whistle in the back pocket. Check out the high backed thermo-molded backrests from Surf to Summit and Ocean Kayak.

Backrest Rodholders

Surf to Summit makes a high quality thermomolded backrest, but a new model coming out soon will be of special interest to kayakfishermen. It has two rodholders built into the back panel. The rodholders are holster style with PVC inserts and are reportedly sturdy enough to use while trolling. At the time of this writing, it is not yet available, but it should be on the market very soon.

Coolers

Coolers are a great multiple use addition to any kayak. They can store your tackle, extra clothing, keys, wallet, cameras, lunch, drinks and bait. You can even use it as a livebait tank. Rodholders can be fastened to the side to create rod storage. When positioned behind your seat, a cooler acts as an additional backrest. A number of kayak firms now have models which have molded-in areas to place a cooler. Smaller coolers can be placed inside the interior of sit-on-bottom kayaks. Most kayaks can be customized to accept a cooler if you do not mind cutting into the hull.

Bow lines

With one end attached to the bow and the other end attached to your belt, you have protection against being separated from your kayak should you take a spill. Also with the bowline attached to your belt, you can wadefish and pull the kayak along behind you with all of your gear. It can also be used as a mooring line when you need to tie up to a dock or a tree limb. By connecting kayaks from bow to stern, you can tow another kayak along which really helps if you have a younger paddler along for the ride. The bowline is a great adjustable length handle when pulling your kayak along on a kayak cart.

Belt

A waterproof belt is very useful as a safety device. You can attach your bowline to it in order to prevent yourself from being separated from your kayak in the event of a spill. Also you can wrap your belt around the upper end of your waders to keep water from seeping in. Also, it is useful to attach the bowline to your belt while wading in order to tow your kayak along. You can make your own wading belt very cheaply by going to your hardware store. Buy enough 1 inch nylon web belt material to go around your waist, and then buy a set of quick interconnecting plastic buckles.

Anchors

Anchors keep kayakfishing efficient on windy days, especially when you've already found the fish. You don't want to drift away once you know where they are hiding. If you get a folding anchor, you can also adjust the anchor for controlled drifting. Small folding anchors of about 1 lb. are perfect. They are available at most marine supply stores, marine supply catalogues such as West Marine Inc. and also at the Coastal Kayakfishing website.

Drag chain

A drag chain is useful when you do not wish to anchor up but wish to drift at a controlled rate. Once you have a section of chain that seems right for your kayak, you can adjust the length of the rope to control your drift rate, according to how much wind or current is present. A chain can even bring your kayak to a complete halt if you lengthen the rope enough. The greatest advantage of the chain over an anchor is the chain's ability to slip over logs and rocks without hanging up. You can pick up a chain and a rope at your local hardware store. If you also attach an interchangeable link to the rope, then you can switch back and forth between the chain and an anchor as needed.

Wading with a bow line

Folding anchors

Rudders

If you paddle a longer kayak, you will especially appreciate rudders. Rudders will allow you to turn your kayak faster using only your feet. Of course, the combination of paddles and rudders is even quicker and more efficient. If your kayak is a smaller more maneuverable kayak of about 12 feet or less, you may not want to bother with installing rudders. But on kayaks of 14 feet or more, they can be a great aid, especially when making maneuvers while fighting a fish. They are also helpful when paddling in a crosswind or for controlling your drift angle when drifting downwind while fishing.

Paddle clips/paddle holder

Paddle holders are at least a convenience, especially if you are anchored up and do not need to be paddling or holding your paddle in your lap. However, when you are coming in for a beach landing, a paddle clip that doubles as a rodholder is practically a must. Your regular upright rodholders will not protect your rods in the event of an overturn which is highly possible when launching or landing in the surf. A great paddle clip that also holds rods securely is available at the Ocean Kayak and Coastal Kayakfishing websites. For sit-on-bottom kayaks, Mark Ambrozic of I.I. Endeavors has a patented paddle/rodholder for sit-on-bottom kayaks called the First Mate at his wewbsite.

Paddleclip/rodholders

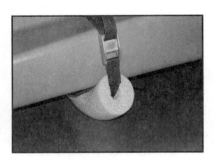

Noodle cartop carriers

Rodholders

There are many styles of rod holders that can be installed on kayaks. Most rodholders that are on the market for conventional boats can be installed permanently or temporarily to either the kayak itself or to a cooler or other fixture such as a milk crate that can be removed from the kayak. Rodholders can be installed that are flushmounted, horizontally deck mounted, or in an upright position. Some new styles of rodholders have been designed specifically for kayakfishing such as the Spike Strike and First Mate. Some rodholders are combination paddle holders such as the paddle clip from Ocean Kayak and the First Mate from I.I. Endeavors (see also Chapter 6: *Customize Your Kayak*).

Backrest Rodholders

Surf to Summit makes a high quality thermomolded backrest, but a new model coming out soon will be of special interest to kayakfishermen. It has two rodholders built into the back panel. The rodholders are holster style with PVC inserts and are reportedly sturdy enough to use while trolling.

Rod savers

Rodsavers are a popular patented set of rodholders often installed on conventional boats to hold rods in position lying horizontal on the deck. They are valuable to kayakfishermen not only as rodholders but also as paddle holders. They can also hold many types of accessory lines in position such as anchor lines, sea anchors, trolling buckets, et cetera. Rodsavers can be purchased at most marine supply stores, marine supply catalogues, and fishing supply catalogues such as Bass Pro Shops.

Knee Straps

Sometimes called knee braces, these straps are very useful when launching or returning in the surf. They help to hold you into the kayak in turbulent water by bracing your knees against them.

Cartop carriers- standard

Standard cartop carriers work just fine for transporting your kayak. If you have kayaks that have the *stacking ability* as one of their features, you will be able to carry as many as six kayaks safely on the top. Standard cartop carriers usually require rain gutters to attach the fasteners to your roof.

Cartop carriers- foam

Foam cartop carriers are great. They fit almost any style of vehicle roof. They are especially helpful when your vehicle does not have the rain gutters where standard cartop carriers normally attach (see photo on page 115). You can attach the foam cushions while the kayak is still on the ground. In fact, you can leave the cushions attached while the kayak is in storage in your garage. You can buy foam cartop carriers at most canoe and kayak dealers and rentals, marine supply stores and catalogues, and on the Internet at the Ocean Kayak website. You can also make your own very economical foam cartop carriers from the foam swimming noodles mentioned so often in this book. You simply need to run a tie down strap through the center of a noodle that has a hole bored through the center (see photo on page 100).

Ocean Kayak cart

RHYNOBAR

Kayak Carts

When you cannot get your vehicle to the water, do not or want to use your vehicle or may not even have a vehicle, a kayak cart may solve your transport problems in getting your kayak to the water. A kayak cart can turn your kayak into a wagon that will also carry all of your gear in one trip. There are a number of different designs and price ranges, including the economical option to make your own. There are some quality commercial kayak carts on the market. Roleez has a kayak cart, the Toteez II, that has wide pneumatic *all-terrain* tires. They will also sell you just the tires if you want to build your own. The wide all-terrain tires are the ultimate choice if you will be rolling your cart over deep, soft sand. Ocean Kayak also has a very nice collapsible cart with reasonably wide tires. The Coastal Kayakfishing website has a kayak cart for sale that will come apart to allow you to stow it below the deck. The Montura Sports Co. has a fully adjustable kayak cart that has scupper hole attachments for sit-on-top kayaks. Some kayak carts on the market, in particular some of the more modestly priced models, have lawnmower wheels or their equivalent for rolling the weight of the kayak. On most surfaces they work fine, but on soft sand, they sink in and drag. Smaller wheels, however, are easier to stow in your kayak. Many kayakers are nervous about leaving an expensive kayak cart sit unattended on the beach while they are out fishing (see also Chapter 8: *Transporting Your Kayak*).

RHYNOBAR

One of the problems often encountered by kayakfishermen who are customizing their kayaks is the challenge of finding suitable attachment sites for all of the accessories that make kayakfishing an efficient endeavor. The various kayak model designs, shapes, and contours present unique challenges to those attempting to customize them. Jeff Krieger designed his RHYNOBAR to create attachment sites on sit-on-top kayaks. It is a stainless steel flat bar that spans the width of your kayak. Mounted forward of the paddler, it is a great place to solidly attach items such as depthfinders and rodholders. Some anglers even use it as a place to attach a rope for towing large fish back to shore when they are too large to haul onboard the kayak.

Depthfinder

A depthfinder/fishfinder can be mounted on your kayak to help you find suspended schools of fish in deeper water. It will also help you to find fish holding structure on the bottom. Use a lighter weight lawnmower battery to save weight. To mount your depthfinder check out the Rhynobar at their website or at Coastal Kayakfishing. To mount your transducer to your hull on a polyethylene plastic kayak, try using a generous amount of 3M 4200 Marine adhesive in white as recommended by a contributor to the Yakfishing.com message board on the Internet. The transducer will be removable. Another contributor recommends Aquaseal from surf and dive shops. You should first sand and wipe with alcohol before applying.

Livewells

There are many commercial livewells on the market that come in many styles and sizes (see also Chapter 12: *Kayak Live Bait Fishing*). Some are polyethylene containers molded specifically for the purpose. Others are varoius types of buckets. Some manufacturers simply fit an aerator to a cooler. You can buy a ready made livewell setup that fits your kayak or you can buy a livewell container, bucket, or cooler separately and choose from a number of aerator types to customize your own setup. The tricky part is getting a container that will fit somewhere convenient on your kayak. The most convenient setup is a kayak that has a molded-in area to accept a cooler. Some of the fish and dive models of sit-on-top kayaks have such an area just behind the seat. Simply find a cooler that matches the dimensions. Usually straps are provided by the manufacturer to hold the cooler in place. If not, it is a simple matter to install them with a rivet gun. If you do not have a cooler space but do have a large hatch opening, you might consider setting a five gallon bucket in the hatch opening and altering the hatch cover with a circular cut out to match the five gallon bucket diameter. Get a bucket with a lid to keep the water from splashing out and your bait from jumping out. Kayak hulls can also be altered to accept a cooler if you are not squeamish about cutting into your kayak.

Aerators

Small bilge pumps that pump water at about 400 gallons per hour are commonly used as aerators. This recirculating type aerator pumps water from the reservoir up a tube and out through small holes drilled into a PVC pipe. The jets of water streaming out the holes drive air down into the water of the reservoir, dissolving air into the water in the process. Bilge pumps run on 12 volt DC batteries. You can use a small RV or lawnmower deep cycle battery, and you can use the same battery to power a depthfinder if you mount one on your kayak. Bait Saver is a well known brand that markets this type aerator as well as other designs and complete livewell systems.

Airstone aerators are simple and do not clog as recirculating pumps often do. Many of them can be run on one or two D cell batteries which makes them very convenient for kayakers. Some units will also run on 12 volt batteries and even house current when you get back home. They consist of a motor that forces air into an air tube and an airstone which diffuses the air into the water in the bait tank.

A newer hybrid system that is known as an air induction system creates a fine mist of air bubbles by sucking air into a tube and mixing it with water being pumped through the system. The force of the infusion of bubbles can be adjusted for more delicate baits. The tiny bubbles make it a good choice for high metabolism saltwater baits. They work on a 12 volt battery. A company called Keep Alive markets this aeration system. A company named Aquatic Ecosystems carries all of the above systems plus many more in their catalogue.

If you do not want to mess with electricity or even air, but want to deliver fresh pure oxygen to your bait, check out The Oxygen Edge from Oxygenation Systems of Texas. The great advantage to kayakfishermen is that the system is quiet delivery of oxygen. Other aeration systems can be pretty noisey compared to the silent characteristics of a kayak, and with this system, you do not have to mess with any batteries. Cabela's sells this system, but if you want to contact the company directly, look for the contact information in the Kayakfishing Resources chapter of this book.

Bait bucket

A trolling bait bucket will allow water to pass through it when immersed in the water, allowing an exchange of water with the lake or ocean water. In this manner your bait will get a constant replenishment of fresh oxygenated water. With the bucket over-board, it is a hindrance to efficient paddling, but it will allow slow paddling. Actually, faster paddling would cause enough stress to bring about the mortality of many live baitfish. A trolling bucket has a lower portion with no holes, so that when stood upright, it will retain about half its original volume of water. This feature will allow you to bring the trolling bucket into the kayak for short periods of time while you paddle harder if needed. Do not forget to occasionally dip the bucket into the water to refresh the small amount of water volume available to the baitfish. A troll-ing bucket works pretty well for a few large and tough baitfish while on the water, but it does not aid in the transport of bait over land before reaching your fishing destination. However, if you have a bait tank in your vehicle with an aeration system or if you can buy your bait in oxygenated bags, a trolling bucket may be all you need. Another alternative would be to catch your bait at your fishing location. Trolling buckets are available at most bait and tackle shops.

Castnet

A castnet is easy to store in your kayak, and it will give you the ability to catch your own fresh livebait on location where you are fishing whenever the oppurtunity arises. If bait is plentiful enough, you will not even need a trolling bucket. You can hook a fresh bait on your hook as you catch it. Castnets are widely avail-able at tackleshops and in tackle supply catalogues. The Aquatic Ecosystems catalogue has all your bait catching and keeping prod-uct needs in one location.

Sea anchors

Sea anchors are used to slow your drift or to control your drift angle. They come in different sizes and more than one can be used at a time. They can be attached to various points along your kayak via quick connect clips to the eyelets. Sea anchors are avail-able in most marine and fishing tackle supply stores, catalogues, and at the Coastal Kayakfishing website.

Dry bags

There are some good quality dry bags on the market that really do keep your water sensitive valuables dry. They work very well for expensive and water sensitive items such as cameras. Dry bags come in a variety of sizes. They are carried by most kayak dealers and are available online at the Ocean Kayak website, Action Watersports, and the Coastal Kayakfishing website which has a large variety of sizes and styles. Waterproof dry boxes are also available.

Insulated bags

Insulated bags are designed to take the place of an insulated cooler when you do not have a convenient place to place a cooler. An insulated bag can conform to the shape and the space that you have available. They are waterproof which means that you can load them up with ice, and they will not leak water into your kayak. They are great for storing your lunch, cold drinks, or your catch below decks, leaving your regular cooler available as a livebaitwell or other storage. They also raise some interesting possibilities as a below deck irregularly shaped livewell. Muleworks, Inc. sells a 22x12x9 inch bag named the Icemule. A three or four foot long bag for cooling larger fish below decks is a product that would really solve a problem for many big fish kayakfishermen.

Noodles

Foam noodles. Fun noodles. Swimming noodles. No matter what you call them, these noodles are very useful to kayakfishermen. You can stuff them into your kayak to make it unsinkable. You can roll your kayak on them around your garage, down the driveway or through the woods. You can set your kayak on them as a cushion while storing your kayak. You can make an economical set of cartop carriers with them. One of the cartop carriers can also double as a kayak sling (see also Chapter 8: *Transporting Your Kayak*). If you are a flyfisherman, you may want to make a flyfishing stripping basket/fish net/fish retainer (see Chapter 10: *Kayak Flyfishing*). If you like to swim from your kayak, do what the kids do. Just have fun with them.

Bunji Cords

Bunji cords have multiple uses in a kayak. You should always have a few onboard. They are useful to hold your kayak in position in a pickup truck bed, on a larger boat deck, or on standard cartop carriers. They are also useful for holding gear and rods in position on your fully loaded kayak while underway in your pickup truck or other vehicle. Also when you want to keep a kayak fully loaded on the deck of a larger boat while speeding through rough water to a fishing destination. When used in combination with eyelets strategically placed around your kayak deck, they can help to hold almost anything in place that you do not wish to fall overboard while fishing, including soft tackle bags, life preservers, coolers or fishing rods.

Nets

Nets can really get in the way in any boat, but they sure are a help when a fish is at the side of your kayak, and you want to get it under control. If you want to store a net out of the way, install an extra rodholder behind your seat where it will not interfere with your upright rods in holders but will still be within reach when you need it. Consider making a flyrod stripping basket/ landing net even if you do not flyfish (see Chapter 10: *Kayakflyfishing*). It works very well as a landing net and also as a live fish holder while you are getting your camera or your pliers. It stows very nicely behind your seat and will work well as an extra cushion if you have a cooler to lean back on.

Gaffs

Short hand gaffs are convenient and do not take up much room, but if you want to control large or dangerous fish from a bit safer distance, use a two handed gaff. Store it in a rodholder behind your seat until you need it. You may want to consider a flying gaff which will detach from the handle and allow the fish to be controlled by a rope. However, you should install a float on your rope to allow you to release it if the fish becomes too wild. You can pick it up again later when the fish calms down. Since flying gaffs are barbed, you can avoid bringing a dangerous fish such as a shark into the boat. Instead, you can drag the fish backward, which will usually kill it, to the nearest beach.

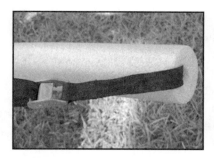
Foam noodle with strap

The Lipper fish gripper

Kayak sling

When the terrain is too rugged for a cart or if you do not have a cart, you can make a kayak sling to help you carry your kayak. The sling is simply a tie down strap that attaches to your kayak and goes over your shoulder for support. A bit of padding in the shoulder area helps to prevent the strap from digging into your shoulder (see also Chapter 8: *Transporting Your Kayak*).

Fish Gripper

There are some specialty tools on the market for grabbing the jaw of a fish with a mechanized device which multiplies the gripping power of your hand. It also protects your hand from any sharp teeth or treble hooks that would do damage to your hand if you tried to grab the fish without the device. One such tool is The Lipper. It takes up very little room in the kayak, but it can make dealing with the fish a lot less complicated and dangerous. The Lipper is sold at Cabela's or you can contact the company directly.

Pliers

Even if you have such a tool as a gripping device, you want to have a set of needlenose pliers. In fact, you want to have a set of needlenose pliers even if you do not have a gripping device. Sometimes it is nearly impossible to pull a hook out with your bare hands or fingers, but a set of needlenose pliers will pop it right out. Don't go out without them. You can get them wherever fishing tackle or hardware supplies are sold.

Forceps

When the hook you want to remove is small to very small, or when the mouth of the fish is very small, you may want to use a pair of forceps which will allow you to remove the smaller hook more easily. Delicate fish such as trout are more carefully handled with forceps. They are perfect for removing tiny flies from the mouths of trout and bluegill.

Measuring tapes

If you want to keep some fish, you should have a measuring tape onboard to make certain you are within legal size restrictions. Even if you plan to release your fish, you may want to satisfy your curiosity. A waterproof ribbon type measuring tape can be purchased at a sewing store. Tackle shops often sell stick on type measuring scales. However, the glue does not stick well to the plastic on kayaks and tends to peel off. A better idea would be a measuring scale drawn with a permanent marking pen with the significant waypoints highlighted.

Cameras

A camera is a good idea to record some significant catches, but you will need to protect it from water. It should be placed into a dry bag and then inside another dry bag or a dry cooler. A waterproof camera would be better yet.

Binoculars

Binoculars are great to have on board. They can help you spot your waypoints forward and behind when paddling longer distances. They are especially helpful for spotting fishy activity at a distance. They can save you a long paddle just to have a look at something with potential. And of course, they can be a lot of fun for looking at the wildlife.

Safety epquipment

Life preservers are one of those things you just have to have on board. Get a very comfortable design so that you will wear it, but make sure that it is a U.S. Coast Guard approved design. A compass will assure you that you are traveling in the right direction, especially in the fog. A GPS unit is nice and can do much in the way of pinpointing waypoints and hidden past fishing holes, but compasses are cheap and you should still have one onboard as a backup. If you have two onboard, you can precisely pinpoint your position on a navigation map. A cell phone is a popular item now, but remember that they do not work everywhere. A whistle or sound making device is one of the required safety items, but it is a good idea to carry a couple flares too. They do not take up much room. If you are going to be out in hot weather, make sure that you have plenty of drinking water and make sure that you take the time to actually drink it. Make sure that you have a first aid kit onboard. Sooner or later you will need it. A bandaid is no big deal unless you do not have one when you need it, especially if you have any kids along for the fun. Always have a good dependable flashlite onboard. Even if you do not plan to be on the water after dark, you may find yourself running late one evening due to unforseen circumstances. Even in the evening, a flashlite is a visual aid to avoid being struck by a larger motorized craft that may not notice you in the low light conditions. After dark, it is frightening to be without a flashlite and to hear a boat engine or see running lights approaching. Make sure your batteries are fresh and your light is working before your trip. An hour or so before evening check your flashlite again.

Sunglasses

Sunglasses are a comfort item, a health concern and a fishing aid. Bright sunshine can be both painful and annoying. It can cause you to squint. Hours of squinting can build up tension, giving you a headache. Headaches can destroy your enjoyment of an otherwise great fishing day. Ultraviolet rays can even be damaging to your eyes. Choose a pair of sunglasses that are dark enough for the brightest sunny days. You can carry another pair for darker days. Get a pair that protects against ultraviolet rays and that are polarized. Polarization will cut down on surface glare on the water, allowing you to see those fish that are swimming right near your kayak unafraid of your presence.

Sunblock

Don't wait. Put it on. Now. What are you waiting for?

Kayakfishing Apparrel

You may want to invest in some special clothing for your comfort, convenience and protection from the sun, heat, wet and cold. Clothing choices are more of a consideration to sit-on-top kayakfishermen than sit-on-bottom fishermen because the sit-on-bottom kayaks have more protection from the elements. With a spray skirt in place, SOB's keep the kayaker dry from the waist down. SOT's, on the other hand, get kayakers wetter from the waist down. In hot weather, getting wet is usually considered a good thing. In cold weather, it can get you a case of hypothermia.

In hot weather or cold, you should wear a hat. In cold weather you can lose 80 per cent of your body heat through your head. In hot weather, you could get sunstroke without a hat. Baseball caps are popular, but they do not protect your ears from the sun. New lightweight synthetic materials allow fishermen to cover up their skin with long pants and long sleeves and still stay cool even out in the hottest weather. The new clothing designs allow air to flow through them, dry quickly after getting wet, and are loose and easy to move in. They have large useful pockets and are available by one brand name or another in almost all larger fishing tackle catalogues, especially those catering to flats or saltwater flyfishermen. Tarponwear and Bonefish Scrubs are two brand name examples of this category of hot weather clothing.

For cool weather wear, many kayakers like to wear wetsuits to give them the insulation to keep warm. Neoprene waders with wade booties and a light rain jacket will give you enough freedom of movement and keep you warm and dry. You can add peel off sweatshirts underneath to add warmth. Sometimes a water resistant windbreaker will shed enough water if it is not raining. Paddling and outdoor gear stores sell specialty dry and wet wear clothing to deal with cool, wet weather and wet environments. Some of this specialty clothing will whisk moisture away from the surface of your skin and allow it to evaporate on the outer surface. Many new styles are designed to fit you like a second skin and have names like Navskin, Second Skin, and Fuzzy Rubber. Among the various types are paddling jackets, pants, short and long sleeve T-shirts (see Chapter 17: *Kayakfishing Resources*).

Chapter Eight

Transporting Your Kayak

Foam cartop carriers

One of the nicest things about a kayak is the elimination of the need for a trailer, and along with the trailer a number of hassles and expenses are also eliminated. The hassle and expense of trailer registration are the first to go, and there is no more trailer insurance. You will not have to wince at destructive corrosion to various trailer parts. In fact, there will be no more trailer maintenance or expensive repairs. No more overheated trailer bearings or flat trailer tires on the road. No more fooling with wiring and faulty trailer lights or police officers in strange towns at 5:00 AM. Also subtract a few tickets from that expense list. Without towing a trailer, you have a reduced chance of accidents. Driving and parking are much easier. You do not need a boat ramp, so you don't pay launch fees. You can launch anywhere that you can get your kayak to the water. So, without a trailer, how do you get your kayak to the water?

Rolling on noodles

To the vehicle

Well, you'll start by getting the kayak to your vehicle, then overland to a body of water, from your vehicle to the body of water, from one body of water to another, and sometimes even across larger bodies of water. Most kayaks are light enough to carry them to your vehicle, but there are alternatives. You can go to Walmart or Kmart and get a couple of those colorful foam swimming pool noodles. If you set a couple under and in front of your kayak, you will be able to effortlessly roll your kayak to your vehicle. Concrete floors or driveways will not damage the bottom of your hull. In fact, you can use the noodles to roll your kayak fully loaded with your gear over stony ground. At home, you can leave your kayak setting on the noodles as a cushions, and while on the water, you can store them inside your kayak. A few noodles inside your kayak will render it unsinkable.

Over land

You can also use noodles to make a set of cartop carrier cushions. Some noodle designs have a small hole bored through the center of their length. You can insert a nylon tie down strap into the hole and pull it through. The noodles are long enough to cut in half and make a pair. Of course, you can buy commercial foam cartop carriers that will have a bit more foam, but they will be a great deal more expensive, and you will not be able to roll your kayak on them. Foam cartop carriers are a good alternative for vehicles that are difficult or impossible to attach to standard removable cartop carriers that require the rain gutters to attach the clamps. For sports utility vehicles that have permanent hard plastic and metal roof racks, a couple of noodles can be fitted over the racks to soften their contact with your kayak. Simply slice them laterally and fasten them to the rack with plastic lock fasteners.

Cartopping is not the most convenient way to transport your kayak, especially if you are driving a van. Most vans are higher than your average car, requiring more effort to mount the kayak on top. However, vans are one of the most convenient modes of transporting your kayak if you are able to slide the kayak into the back. It really gets convenient if you can leave your kayak sitting on a set of noodles or a kayak cart fully loaded with all of your fishing gear. Then, simply roll it out to your van and slide it into the van upright with all your gear. It only takes a minute. Then, it only takes a minute to slide it back out at the waters edge, and you are on your way fishing. Sometimes it's not so easy getting to the water's edge, especially in rough country. A four wheel drive pickup truck is just as convenient for sliding a fully rigged kayak in and out, and with 4WD and a kayak, you are rigged for just about anywhere. There are some places near civilization, however, that local ordinances or landowner restrictions will prevent you from driving a vehicle to the waters edge. Some coastal towns will not allow vehicles on the beach. Other situations with narrow passages through trees or other obstructions both natural and manmade will require that you leave your vehicle some distance from the water. Rolling on noodles is only practical for short distances. A kayak cart, however, can make the transport an enjoyable experience. A couple of wheels can turn your kayak into a wagon that will transport all of your gear as easily as a walk in the park. However, if you encounter soft sand, mud, or especially rough terrain, you may need a cart with *all-terrain* wheels.

Toteez II all terrain kayak cart

You can buy a commercial kayak cart or build your own. All kayak carts do not fit every design of kayak hull. Some carts are designed for specific kayak designs. Check with the vendor to be sure it fits your make and model kayak. Some commercial carts come with small narrow wheels that are fine for solid ground but will bog down and drag through soft sand. Other commercial carts designed with all-terrain tires work very well on sand and mud but are very expensive and worrisome to leave on the beach while you are out fishing. Some models will come apart quickly so that you can stow them in your kayak hatches. All-terrain tires are much larger though, and you will need large hatch openings to store them inside sit-on-top kayaks. Otherwise, you will need to leave the cart unattended on the shore or walk back to your vehicle to lock it in the relative safety there. When you return from fishing, you will also have to walk up to your vehicle, leaving your kayak at the waters edge until you return with the cart. There is no single solution for all kayakers in all models and all transporting situations. The best solution for you might not meet the needs of the next guy. If you cannot find a commercial kayak cart (see Chapter 17: *Kayakfishing Resources*) that meets at least most of your needs, you can design and build your own (see Building a Kayak Cart at the end of this chapter).

Water to Water

When you want to travel from one body of water to another or from one part of a river to another to avoid rapids or other impassable obstructions, it is called a *portage*. A portage is also useful in areas where there are many bodies of water in close proximity to one another. Sometimes there are small ponds adjacent to larger lakes. Small pond-like areas of a larger lake are sometimes cut off from the main body of water due to a drought. Often these more inaccessible bodies of water are honeyholes worth a little extra effort to get into. Sometimes they are worth a lot of effort.

When the portage is a short distance and the ground is covered with grass, leaves or pine needles, you may just want to grab the bow line and drag your kayak and gear the short distance. Plastic kayaks are very durable and there is usually very little harm in doing so. But where there are pebbles, stones or shells, they can scrape the bottom of your kayak. A heavy canvass tarp can be wrapped around the hull of your kayak to drag over abrasive areas, and it can be easily stored in your kayak. If you are on a camping trip, the tarp will also be useful for many other purposes. Of course, you can also use your foam noodles that are stored below deck for flotation to roll your kayak. Depending upon your determination and patience, you can travel some surprising distances in this manner with little physical exertion. A kayak cart, however, is the ultimate form of transportation in such situations, especially if there is some distance to travel. Of course, a cart that breaks down for storage below deck or that can be strapped out of your way to the deck is required. Obviously, all-terrain tires would be preferrable to smaller, thinner width tires if your kayak has the storage space.

In more rugged areas, where rocks boulders or logs prevent the use of a kayak cart, a kayak sling might prove useful. A kayak sling is a nylon strap that attaches to your kayak and passes over one shoulder in the same manner that a musician wears a guitar strap. The strap transfers some of the weight of the kayak to your

16 yr. old Danielle with fully loaded kayak and no hands

shoulders and legs rather than having your hands and arms bearing the full load. The weight transfer will allow you to carry the load farther and longer. In fact, if you are traveling light enough and have all your gear held in place with straps and bunji cords, you may be able to carry your kayak and all of your gear in one trip, depending upon the weight of your kayak, gear, the distance and your own physical abilities.

The key to making a kayak sling work are the attachment points to the kayak. The scupper holes on many sit-on-top kayaks are excellent places to run the strap through if they will result in proper weight balance. For kayaks that do not have conveniently placed scupper holes and for most sit-on-bottom kayaks, you can add a couple nylon strap brackets with a rivet gun. Simply fasten them equidistant from the center of balance on the port or starboard side of the upper deck above the water line. They are available at most marine supply stores and sold as 12 volt battery tie downs.

The same cartop carrier made from the swimming pool noodles can function as a kayak sling. The foam cushion will keep the strap from cutting into your shoulder and causing you pain. If you would like to make a sling with a smaller diameter foam shoulder cushion, go to your hardware dealer and ask to see some foam insulated pipe covers. The sling can be kept very easily in the storage areas in almost any kayak (see also Chapter 7: *Kayakfishing Accessories*).

Over water

At times you may want to travel by water to fishing areas that are too far and not feasible to paddle by kayak within limited time restraints. You can travel around the world in a kayak, but not on a daytrip. A kayak rigged, ready to fish and strapped to the deck of a larger boat is a great way to get to some of that distant water that would be great to fish by kayak, but you just don't have the travel time.

Building a Kayak Cart

When the commercial entities that be are not meeting the needs or have not caught up with the needs of imaginative and deter-mined people, the people usually exercise innovative abilities and invent the solution to their own particular needs. Many times this results in a new commercial entity. A great example is a guy who posted his solution to building a kayak cart to deal with sandy beaches on a fishing bulletin board. He used a pair of kids water skis attached to the bottom of his cart to slide his cart over the sand to the waters edge. He didn't go into detail, but somehow the wheels folded up out of the way when the skis were in use. I'm guessing that he had to leave that Cadillac of kayak carts at the beach while he was out fishing. Since it was made from inex-pensive materials from a yard sale and home depot, he probably didn't get too nervous about it. No one but Santa Claus delivering Christmas toys in the desert would steal it.

Home made kayak cart

I read a bulletin board posting on the Internet from a guy who made a kayak cart from PVC pipe, an axle, and an old pair of lawnmower wheels. He didn't give many design details, but the crucial factor that made the design work well was that the PVC passed up through the scupper holes to hold the kayak cart in position under the kayak. I do not know how closely my cart resembles the design of the author of the bulletin board posting, but as a result of the posting, the cart I designed for an Ocean Kayak *Scrambler XT* is simple, easy to use, effective, convenient, and easy to make. It has a wagon-like ability to cart along all my fishing tackle and gear, and it tows nicely by adjusting the length of my bowline.

Loaded kayak on cart

Homemade PVC cart

It also attaches to the top deck of my kayak out of the way behind the seat where it does not interfere with fishing or paddling (see photo on page 95). It rests on the gunnels in a pair of recessions meant to place a paddle at rest behind the seat. It is held in place on top of the kayak by two 90 degree vertical projections of PVC which lay on either side of the thermomolded seat and the quick connect straps behind the seat that fasten the seat to the kayak and pass over the axle. It is the most convenient kayak cart because you can take it out on the water with you without breaking it down or reassembling it when you return to shore. When the terrain is very bumpy and rough, you can attach a rubber bunji cord to the axel, over the kayak and back to the axel on the other side. The cord will prevent the upright projections from popping out of the scupper holes, but the bunji cord is rarely needed. Although the lawnmower wheels will pass through a moderate amount of soft sand, all-terrain tires can be substituted if you encounter deep, soft sand on a regular basis. If you drill a hole on each end of the axel and use removeable pins instead of tap-on axel end caps to hold the wheels on, you will be able to interchange between wider all terrain tires and the smaller lawnmower tires. You will also be able to break the cart down to stow it below deck if you want. You will need a longer axle for the wider all-terrain tires, and you will need PVC spacers on the axel when using the thinner lawnmower tires. The cart will be easier to stow below the deck inside of the hatches when using the smaller lawnmower wheels.

Roleez all terrain tire

All terrain tire track

Sit-on-bottom kayak cart

To make a simple kayak cart for a sit-on-bottom kayak, you will need an axle long enough that the wheels when attached to the axle will not rub the sides of the kayak. You will need a piece of PVC pipe to cover the axle. Since there are no scupper holes, you will not need the upright sections of PVC pipe. You will need to attach the PVC covered axle to a length of 2x4 lumber, according to the width of your kayak and leaving enough space for the wheels. You can use pipe fasteners which are available in most hardware stores to fasten the axle and PVC pipe to the 2x4. On the opposite side of the 2x4 you will need a heavy piece foam attached to cushion your kayak hull. In order to hold the kayak in position on the cart, you will need a very tight nylon adjustable strap. To fasten the straps to each end of the 2x4, double over the strap on each end and use wood screws with wide flat washers. Place the cart under the kayak in an area where the strap will not slip off. Tighten the strap enough to make the hull press into the foam, preventing the kayak from slipping off the kart, especially when the wheels encounter obstructions.

Chapter Nine

Kayakfishing Skills and Techniques

Skills pay off

One of the most important factors in catching fish is the efficient use of time and oppurtunity. The more efficiently you use your time, then all the more oppurtunities will be presented to you. Then you must capitalize on those oppurtunities. Basically, it all boils down to keeping your lure or bait in the strike zone. Everything you do on a given day will factor into the formula for how much time your offering spends in front of potential targets.

Therefor, your total skills coming into play in varying environmental conditions and oppurtunistic situations will determine the success you enjoy at catching fish. These skills range from your handling of your kayak, paddles, anchors and other kayak equipment to how well you access and handle your fishing epquipment, especially when presented with one of those oppurtunities.

At-the-ready

Boat positioning

One of the greatest advantages of the kayak over canoes is the ability to leave the double-bladed paddle lay *at-the-ready* in your lap. For the active fisherman, who is on the move casting repeatedly to targets and often changing direction or adjusting position while casting and retrieving, it is the most important advantageous factor in paddlesport fishing. The main reason for the great increase in efficiency for the kayakfisherman is that you don't have to set your fishing pole down or stop fishing to pick up a paddle, oars, or push pole to make adjustments in position, to change direction of drift or to move short distances. Also, after paddling, you do not have to carefully set the paddle down before picking up your fishing pole again to resume fishing, and you do not have to take time to set it down carefully to avoid spooking any fish. These advantages cause the kayakfisherman to become more efficient than a modern day angler epquipped with a trolling motor. The use of trolling motors revolutionized

One hand on the paddle

freshwater fishing many years ago and more recently revolutionized saltwater fishing, but modern day kayaks can be just as efficient or even more so.

In order to capitalize fully on these advantages, a kayak angler should practice utilizing the paddle with one hand while holding the rod in the other hand. Few people can apply a significant amount of pressure with only one hand on the paddle. Using two hands, a paddler pushes or pulls in opposite directions with each hand. An efficient system. Since this technique is impossible with one hand occupied by a fishing pole, the angler needs to find something to be the opposing force at the other end of the paddle. In most cases, an obstruction acting as a pivot point can supply the opposing force which is usually a selected body part. When paddling in reverse, you can use your stomach, solar plexus, or rib cage area for the opposing obstruction (see photo pictured below). Paddle strokes in reverse direction are more often used to correct a drift direction and to slow or stop forward progress than they are used to actually travel in a reverse direction. Going

Solar plexus as a pivot

forward, you can also use your stomach or ribcage area in conjunction with your triceps or rear side of your elbow on the rod hand to trap your paddle at the opposite end from your paddle hand (see top photo on page 129) unless you need more power in which case you will use your forearm or your fist on your rod-clenched hand (see bottom photo on page 129). The closed fist can actually apply quite a bit of forward thrust while the paddle hand pulls backward on the opposite end driving the kayak forward. To continue fishing, simply drop the paddle in your lap. You might want to use these techniques when approaching fish or a casting target, preparing to cast, retrieving lures, trolling live baits, or even when fighting a fish, especially if a strong fish is headed

Triceps and ribcage as a pivot

Clenched rod hand or forearm as a pivot

for an obstruction such as a log, dock pilings or mangroves, and it would be helpful to move in reverse when the fish is pulling your kayak ever closer to the obstruction, despite a locked down drag. Your only other alternatives would be to quickly throw the anchor overboard or use a stakeout technique such as kayakfishing guides Capt. Allen Cartmell or John Stanton use (see Chapter 16: *Kayakfishing Experts*).

Paddle leash

With all of the excitement of casting, retrieving and hopefully fighting fish, it is probable that at some point a paddle is going to fall from your lap and go overboard. This could be an unfortunate situation, even more so, if a big fish is towing you in the opposite direction. For that reason, you should attach your paddle to the kayak with a paddle leash. A paddle leash is a short stretching and contracting cord that prevents your paddle from drifting away. With this device in place, you can forget about the paddle. If it falls overboard, then fine. You can put it back into the kayak later. In the meantime, you can concentrate on catching or fighting a fish. After fishing in this manner for some time, it is actually rare for the paddle to actually fall out of your lap and go overboard, but it does afford peace of mind about it. It is almost as easy to pick up a floating paddle overboard on a short stretch leash as it is from your lap or from a paddle holder. Paddle holders are convenient, but they can be inefficient compared to the *paddle-on-the-lap technique*. As an attachment that projects out from the kayak, their placement can sometimes interfere with paddling. For a flyfisherman, it is one more potential hazard to catch on loose coils of flyline. If you paddle to a location to fish and then fish at anchor or do not have further need of the paddle, then you may warrant its use as a convenience. Surf launching kayakfishermen like to use paddle holders that double as rodholders when launching or returning to the beach because their rods are firmly secured in the event of an overturn in the surf. On some higher floating sit-on-top models and most sit-on-bottom kayaks, your lap is not available or convenient as a paddleholder.

Sprint paddling

Generally, as a kayakfishermen you should pace yourself while paddling and use a lightweight moderately bladed paddle. You can travel further and average better time if you paddle at a steady pace that will not eventually exhaust you. In fact, you should plan your fishing day and environment where you can fish and paddle interchangeably throughout your fishing day rather than traveling a long distance to the fishing site. Your paddling will then be less like work and more efficient and enjoyable. However, there are exceptions. At some locations and times, there is a high probability of *schooling fish* attacking bait at the surface. Often the action is consistent and frequent enough that a kayakfisherman can spend hours of exciting fishing time *sprint paddling* from one surfacing school to another. They usually pop up on the surface for short periods of time in an unpredictable pattern as they ambush schools of baitfish and then disappear. The surface blitz can last a few minutes to a few hours. It can involve a few fish or thousands. The fish can be large and/or small, and it can be a multiple species event. In any case, you want to get there as quickly as possible. A kayak paddle with a larger blade surface will get you to those shorter distance oppurtunities much faster. On days when I expect such activity is probable, I will carry the larger bladed paddle. Also, on river paddling excursions where quick powerful adjustments to the direction of travel are more important than stamina, I will carry the power paddle. In some situations, your need for a power stroke to avoid striking rocks and logs or to avoid being swept underneath overhanging tree limbs while traveling downstream with a current is your primary paddling challenge.

Drifting Techniques

Generally speaking, you can locate more fish by kayak while drifting, especially when you are covering a large open water area of an unvarying type. In other words, when a fish has no obvious (to you) reason to be in one area over another. After covering some amount of water, you may discover that there is a noticeable pattern that was not at first obvious to you. Until then, covering water may be the most efficient use of your time. At times, drift fishing across a bay may be your secondary objective, but drifting across it and fishing it is a good investment of time rather than paddling to your primary objective before fishing. In a kayak, you can control the direction of your drift very easily with a minimum of paddling. Your kayak will never stay pointed directly downwind. It will vary to some degree either to the port or starboard. Your progress downwind will lean more to the direction that your kayak is pointed. It will continue in that

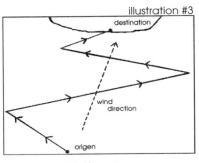

Drift pattern

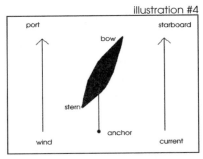

Anchoring rear starboard

direction until you alter the direction it points. Therefor you can drift very precisely to a downwind target although you will not orient or travel directly toward it. You simply change orientation from port to starboard or back again by one backward thrust of the paddle on either side of the kayak. By adjusting the length of time you travel at each orientation, you can control your eventual destination downwind with a minimum of paddlework. You will travel a *zig zag pattern* that will give a you a larger and more varied sample of the open water area (see illustration #3). Most important, however, you will get to fish the water very efficiently with a minimum of paddling effort. This method works well whether using artificial lures or live bait. In fact, a very efficient method of fishing involves the use of a live baitfish under a float drifting out the back of the kayak while fan casting artificials in all directions.

Sea Anchors

Sea anchors are great for slowing or controlling your drift as well as controlling the position or angle of your kayak with repect to the wind or current. Sea anchors come in different sizes which can be used according to how much drag resistance you need. More than one can be used together to create increased drag. They can be placed anywhere on your kayak by attaching them to the eyelets to control the drift angle. They can be attached according to illustrations #4, 5 and 6 for the desired effect.

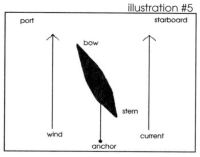

Anchoring rear port

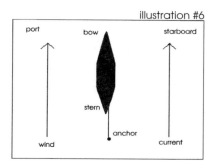

Anchoring off stern

Rudders

Rudders can help you to control your direction of drift or paddling with a minimum of effort. They can be very helpful especially on longer and harder to turn kayaks. If you fish from a *touring* or longer kayak, especially one that may have a bow or stern with a keel that projects down below the surface, your kayak may be difficult to turn or maneuver without rudders. Some kayak models come with rudders. If yours does not, then you may want to consider having one installed. They will allow you to control the kayak via foot pedals that are connected by cable to the rudder.

Controlling drift

Kayaks are very drift resistant compared to canoes and larger motorized craft. However, at times, you may be drifting faster than you would like, especially if you are catching fish from an area. There are a number of ways to control your drift rate. In shallow water, the easiest and most convenient way is to use a small folding anchor (see photo on page 99 in Chapter 7: *Kayakfishing Accessories*). A folding anchor can be locked in the open tine position or closed position. In the open tine position, the tines will normally catch on the bottom and stop your kayak. Locked in the closed tine position, the kayak will most often drift in a breeze, but more slowly than it would without the closed tine anchor overboard. Of course, if there is no breeze, it may even bring your kayak to a halt, at least temporarily. In light winds, you can use a combination of the closed tine position, drifting, and even light paddling for a controlled and careful advance into a promising area. To add resistance to the anchor, whether in open or closed tine position, lengthen the anchor rope. Sometimes in heavy wind, your kayak will continue to drift even in the open tine position. Lengthening the rope can slow you down or even stop you. In situations where you would like to continue to drift rather than stop, shorten the anchor rope. In some environments with a rough bottom, the open tine or even closed tine anchor will hang up on the bottom and prevent any drifting. Rock and log strewn bottoms can sometimes even be a nuisance to retrieving your anchor. To remedy the situation, a kayak angler can use an old river fisherman's trick. Use a short piece of chain instead of an anchor. Experience will tell you how long or heavy the chain should be in your fishing environment. You can even lengthen or shorten the chain on the water by connecting short lengths of chain with removable links that are available in hardware stores. Also, once again, you can lengthen or shorten the anchor rope to adjust the amount of drag required. Of course, since this is an old river drift fishing technique, it works as well in river currents as it does in wind.

The anchor rope should be within easy reach and should be set at a length no longer than actually needed to get the job done. In shallow water, it may only need to be a few feet long. A short anchor rope is much easier to pull up and toss into the kayak. In deeper water, you may actually want an anchor winch.

Kayakfishing guides—Capt. Allen Cartmell in Texas and John Stanton in Florida—have adopted similar stakeout techniques instead of using an anchor. Both guides are shallow saltwater flatsfishermen who specialize in redfish. Capt. Cartmell uses a wooden stake with a sharp end that passes through a scupper hole on a sit-on-top kayak and penetrates the sand or mud bottom, stabilizing the kayak in a stationary position. John Stanton uses a 3/16 by 36 inch aluminum rod. He sharpens one end and drills a 1/8 inch hole through the other end. He places a stainless steel ring through the hole and attaches a four foot rope. On the other end of the rope he attaches a brass clip. He uses the clip to attach the stake to his kayak or to his belt loop. He does not use a scupper hole but places the stake outside the kayak. When staking outside the kayak, a paddle leash with a retractible cord makes a convenient tether for your stake, and when the bottom is soft enough, your paddle can sometimes be used as a stake if you do not have a one. It can be more convenient, efficient and less messy than an anchor.

Another old river fisherman's technique substitutes a large clamp attached to a short cord instead of an anchor and rope. Instead of dropping an anchor down into heavy, messy muck bottoms, the clamp attaches to tree limbs, log jams, lily pads, other surface vegetation, or anything you can get between the jaws of the clamp. It can be very quick and convenient compared to an anchor in many situations where an anchor might hang up regularly or simply take more time to raise and lower.

Where you attach your anchor rope will effect the position of your kayak with respect to the wind drift or current. Anchoring on the rear starboard side will leave the port side facing slightly downwind or downcurrent (see illustration #4) which is an advantageous angle for casting at targets downwind or on the port side. Likewise, a rear port side anchor point will leave the starboard side to the downwind or down current side of the kayak (illustration #5). If you want the bow of the kayak to hang in the current or breeze directly downstream or downwind, then the contact point should be at the tip of the stern (see illustration #6). You may have noticed that I didn't say attachment point. Because the stern of the kayak is a difficult point to reach to either attach or detach the anchor rope while sitting in the kayak, you want to use an open ended cleat to guide the line to the stern. With an attachment point just behind the seat, you will be able reach the rope easily and guide it into the open cleat which will restrain it at this point. The cleat will serve the same purpose as an attachment point, but you will be able to guide it out of the open ended cleat at the stern from your seated position in the kayak. Rather than use a metal or plastic open cleat, you should use the softer but tough rubber cleats that can mold to the contour of the point you want to place it. With the rubber cleats, you can force the anchor rope into and out of the opening much more easily. In order to orient the the bow of the kayak upwind or upsteam, you would want the attachment point or cleat forward toward the bow but accessible from your position.

Tommy Stubbs of Beaumont, Texas is into kayak rigging, and he installed a movable anchoring system on his kayak. With this system, Tom can pull on his carabiner line and change the anchor attachment site to any point on his kayak from bow to stern. He can orient his kayak in any position with respect to wind or current.

Fishing Upwind

One of the most difficult fishing situations occurs when you need to travel and cast artificials upcurrent or upwind. The stronger the wind or current becomes, the less efficient the kayakfisherman becomes. The reason is that more effort must be made with the paddle to maintain position or advance toward casting targets. To maintain your fishing efficiency you will need to employ a few tricks or make some basic technique changes. One of the most convenient tricks is to use heavy vegetation of some type: either heavily matted surface vegetation or heavily emergent vegetation. You paddle up onto matted vegetation. If the wind is not too strong, it will hold you in place while you cast to surrounding waters before paddling further upwind or current to the next clump of vegetation. Paddling just upwind of a thick patch of reeds and then allowing the kayak to blow back against them will often hold the kayak in position during heavy winds. Thick lily pads and spatterdocks will usually work as long as the winds are not too strong. Sometimes logs are helpful, and in the absence of anything else, a shoreline bank can be used by partially grounding the bow of the kayak as you advance. You can also use the quick clip or clamp on the clumps of vegetation to help in holding the kayak in place if the wind is a bit too strong. If the wind is still too strong or if there is no vegetation thick enough to lodge or clamp onto, then you can throw out an anchor. However, if your anchor is fastened to the kayak behind you, then your kayak will eventually swing downwind or current leaving you facing the opposite direction of your target and your direction of travel.

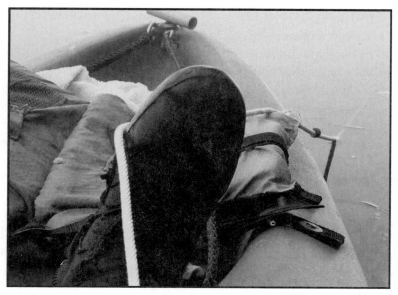

Toe-trick setup

Rather than employing a difficult to reach attachment point at the bow, you can use a *toe trick* to create a temporary forward attachment point and conveniently orient the bow of your kayak upwind or upcurrent. Unfortunately the toe trick only works in a sit-on-top kayak, but you could ad a temporary attachment device to a sit-on-bottom kayak at a forward location where it would be within easy reach. To employ the toe trick, simply paddle upwind or current to the point you want to cast at a target, set the anchor over, but take the rope, reach forward, and place it on the inside of your foot (see photo on page 137). As the current or wind exerts pressure backward on the kayak, the foot creates a perfect temporary restraining point that orients the kayakfisherman upwind or current facing the target area ahead when traveling upwind. It is not as efficient as fishing downwind, but in shallow water where you do not have a long anchor rope to pull up, it can be a very efficient method of traveling and fishing upwind.

Trolling

However, a more relaxing and efficient method of fishing upwind or current would be trolling. A solid rodholder is required, especially when there is a potential for big fish because you probably will not be holding the rod when the fish strikes. Therefor, a good drag—set strong enough to hook the fish but light enough so as not to break the line—is essential. You can troll using live bait or artificial lures. It can be a very relaxing and very effective method of fishing. The key is to avoid hanging up on weeds or bottom obstructions. When fishing live baitfish, it is usually best to use a float which will allow you to slow down or even stop without the baitfish sinking to the bottom and hanging up. Also, a weedless hook is important. The same purpose can be achieved when trolling artificials by using a floating lure that dives when retrieved and returns to the surface when stopped. Of course there are many variations according to species and environmental situations, but the point is to fish effectively and efficiently when you need to fish upwind by maximizing your opputunities to keep your offering in front of the fish. Actually, trolling is also a very effective method of fishing downwind also. In fact, while traveling downwind, you do less paddling and your hands are free to cast artificials with a second rod as you troll (see also Trolling in Chapter 11: *Kayak Lure Fishing* and Chapter 12: *Kayak Live Bait Fishing*).

Wading support

Wading Techniques

Another great way to beat the wind while kayakfishing is to get out of the kayak and wade. Wading is sometimes even more effective than fishing from a kayak or any other craft. Fishing from a kayak is a great way to locate fish, but hopping out and wading is often an even better way to take advantage of a fishing area once the fish are located. While wading, you do not have to be concerned with the paddle or boat positioning. There is no threat of drifting too close or on top of the fish you are trying to catch. You can take all the time necessary to approach a single fish or to adequately fish a particularly fishy area. Wadefishing from a kayak can be even more stealthy and convenient than wadefishing from other craft. The three most important accessories you need are a wading belt, a bowline and a light folding anchor. Of course, a good pair of wading boots and a pair of neoprene waders are nice in cold weather. You will need to attach the bowline to your web belt via a quick release clip at one end and attach the other end to the bow of the kayak. Since the water is shallow, you will need only a short anchor rope. The anchor tines should be in the folded position so that it will create a slight drag but not fully hang up on bottom. In this manner, the kayak will trail neatly behind you as you travel. If winds are light, you can even travel downwind without the kayak trying to blow past you. However, if the winds are strong, you may need to set the tines open on the anchor to keep the kayak trailing behind you. One of the benefits of traveling upwind is that you will probably not need the anchor out at all. Even with the anchor out, if you need any tackle or a bite of your sandwich, just tug on the bowline and it will be at your fingertips in a second. While flyfishing, remember to take down any rods that are standing upright in the rodholders that might catch on your backcast.

Beyond transportation, a kayak is a great wading aid that can greatly enhance wading stability where there are strong tides, downstream currents, or where the bottom is treacherous with deep holes or sharp uneven rocks. By transferring most of your weight onto the kayak and sliding your feet lightly over the uneven terrain, you can glide over the bottom in a manner that you can't imagine without the kayak. Also you can carry much more of everything you might need or want that would have been impossible if wading without the kayak. On smallmouth bass and trout rivers, it sure beats a wading staff.

Sightfishing

Sightfishing is traditionally done from a raised platform. The low perspective of a kayak makes it difficult to see below the surface. Except when fish get close. Too close. Even though fish often swim right by your kayak without spooking, presentations to fish in shallow water are not generally successful at only a rod length away which is often the distance at which you can see an individual fish underwater. However, the low perspective that takes away from underwater visibility, exaggerates other visible cues to the presence of fish. The phenomenon of *nervous water* appears much more obvious when sitting so low on the water. Nervous water is a condition that occurs at the surface when a school of fish is present just below the surface. It is usually much more pronounced when the water surface is very calm. It can be caused by a single fish, but it is much more pronounced when a large school is present. Nervous water is easier to spot in shallow water, in part, because shallow water is usually more calm, but often because the water bulges with the reduced water column forcing the fish so close to the surface that, at times, the fins actually protrude through the surface. This creates an even more enhanced oppurtunity to spot the fish. However, nervous water and even visible fins and tails occur over deeper water also as schools of fish often travel and sometimes even appear to sleep or rest at the surface. Tarpon, cobia, jack crevalles, redfish, ladyfish, bluefish and sharks commonly expose themselves at the surface, and sometimes: black drum and weakfish.

Tails are more commonly spotted in shallow water where the tailing behavior occurs when various species of fish feed on the bottom in water so shallow that their tails stick out of the water when they lean downward to root around for food items. Tailing behavior is most often associated with saltwater fish while flatsfishing for bonefish, redfish, black drum and sheepshead, but in freshwater, large carp also exhibit this behavior and present some very challenging sightfishing oppurtunities. In the spring, largemouth bass tails can often be spotted as they engage in the spawning process. Wherever and whichever tails are spotted, they stick out like someone waving at flag at you. From your low perspective in your kayak, those flags seem to wave a lot higher.

There are other signs to keep a watch for while sightfishing which may not be a sighting of an actual fish. Kayakfishermen should be especially alert for distant reflections at the water surface in bright sunshine, baitfish schools, and birds. Reflections can indicate fish breaking the surface of the water on sunny days. Reflections can help fishermen to spot fish at great distances that would be very difficult or impossible to see without them. The reflections are caused by wet fins, tails, or shiny scales on the body breaking the surface on a sunny day. Even more visible reflections are given off by the splashing of distant feeding fish on the horizon. Sometimes this feeding activity can be very extensive with many fish, multiple species and lasting or reocurring over a period of time. In most cases, this type of activity will at-

Tribalance Kayak

tract birds such as seagulls and terns which will join in the fray. If the lighting conditions are not conducive for reflections, anglers can usually spot the birds flying over the meelee. Sometimes the birds are visibly diving on baitfish that are not visibly under attack by gamefish, but anglers should always investigate such activity. Wherever there is a concentration of baitfish, gamefish invariably show up before long. In fact, baitfish schools can usually be spotted without the birds by watching for them skipping over the surface to avoid the gamefish before the birds even show up. If you want to get in on the action even earlier, try to spot the schools of bait before the predators. They can be spotted by the nervous water they create near the surface in the same manner that gamefish can be spotted. Often there are gamefish below baitfish even though there is no surface evidence of their presence. Sometimes they are hiding in bottom vegetation, ambushing the deeper swimming members of the school, and sometimes they are merely following the baitfish.

Some anglers want the advantages of fishing from a kayak, but refuse to sacrifice their traditional sightfishing methods where they stand to spot the fish underwater. Standing in a kayak is not a mainstream skill. Only the most stable kayaks will allow it. However, one company has developed a kayak designed to do just that. Of course, you can also sit down to paddle or fish. The *Tribalance Kayak* has two small pods on either side of the stern to stabilize it. Kayakfishing guide, John Stanton, has sold all of his traditional kayaks and replaced them with new *Tribalance* kayaks. John specializes in sightfishing for tailing redfish on the Florida flats.

Chapter Ten

Kayak Flyfishing

Kayak wading and flyfishing

This chapter is not intended to teach flyfishing, but instead to enlighten potential kayak flyfishermen in respect to flyfishing from a kayak, to raise some thinking in regards to the dynamics involved, and hopefully, to help a flyfisherman or someone starting out to have more initial success rather than battling with the early experience. There are some important advantages to flyfishing by kayak, and there are also some problems, but the

problems do have solutions. Few flyfishermen seem to have discovered kayaks. Many of the the same people who are drawn to
flyfishing would also be drawn to kayaking. Indeed, some do
both but few at the same time. Perhaps they have not fully considered the advantages, or perhaps they have not worked through
some of the initial problems by trial, error and then eventually to
reward filled experience.

One of the most important advantages to kayak flyfishing is
that it is so enjoyable. Not because it is so convenient and economical, which is certainly true, but because they are fun to paddle
and glide along in many and varied environments viewing nature
along the way. Indeed kayaks have a large following that find no
need for fishing during their day's outing. However, there is just
something about the beauty of kayaking that matches the beauty
of flycasting, and kayaking is easier to learn. Few of us begin our
flyfishing careers in a form that could be described as beautiful,
but with time and persistence, a form of beauty emerges that
brings with it a sense of ease, simplicity and accomplishment
that becomes rewarding and enjoyable beyond other forms of
fishing. First attempts at flyfishing from a kayak, however, might
give a fly angler a sense of struggle and frustration not experienced since their earlier days of learning. Careful consideration
of the factors responsible for the problems will reveal solutions
that will carry a kayak flyfisher to a new level of simplicity, beauty,
accomplishment and enjoyment. These solutions can result in a
higher level of flyfishing through the advantages of efficiency
and stealth.

Kayak flyfishing can be very efficient in repect to covering
lots of water because the slow drifting, light paddling, and occa-
sional anchoring matches well with a flyrod's ability to test
samples of water areas and types without fully retrieving the line
back to the kayak. The flyfisherman's ability to lift line from the
water and drop a fly at another location while steadily moving
along at a controlled pace matches well with a kayak's effortless
wandering at fishable rates of progress. Time on the water is uti-
lized very efficiently in the search process. While moving along
at a controlled but steady pace, spot testing of open water areas,

various openings in weed patches, or of bankside targets such as overhanging bushes and trees, fallen logs, rocks or docks can be accomplished with a minimum of retrieving of the line. In other words, the fly spends more time in the selected potential strike zones. Once a successful pattern is established from the variety of cover and structure situations, the process can be even further streamlined to make presentations to the most productive fish holding cover situations for a given day if there is such a fish preference indicated.

Mountain stream kayak wade flyfishing

Stealth is probably the most commonly appreciated advantage of flyfishing by kayak. A kayak is even stealthier than a canoe. It has a lower visibilty profile, and the material is usually more resistant to accidental noise due to paddle and epquipment handling. Kayaks are especially stealthy in the shallows where bigger boats will scare everything within casting range and sometimes further. In fact, fish rarely act negatively to a kayak's presence and often swim and strike right at boatside. Not only will kayaks get you quietly back into the shallows, but they will often get you back into waters that are inaccessable to larger craft.

Shallows, rocks, oyster bars, logs and heavy weedcover often result in inefficient attempts to fish much beyond the edges of such cover. Larger boat hulls and spinning propellors often have a difficult time fishing such areas without creating fish spooking noises and may be prevented access altogether. Kayaks, however, pass through this type environment effortlessly. Quiet and efficient penetration of shallow water and heavy weedcover by kayak and flyrod are an awsome combination. I do not think that it can be accomplished more efficiently or stealthily any other way. You can get back in there quietly, and your flies can further penetrate shallow, weedy areas, touching down lightly without spooking fish.

The first problem that confronts a flyfisherman attempting to flyfish from a kayak is—*where to put all of the line*. The longer the cast, the bigger the problem. With conventional tackle, the line is stored on a reel between casts, but it is very inconvenient to wind up and restrip flyline between casts. Some flyfishermen are very adept at retrieving and holding flyline in their hand, but this method is not practical in most situations, especially from a moving kayak or on longer casts and faster retrieves which require much arm extension. The line will also need to be dropped when picking up the paddle to move from place to place or to adjust the kayak's position. So, the kayaker must either set the line onboard the kayak or overboard.

Setting line onboard the kayak prevents it from drifting away while anchored in current, drifting in windy situations or while paddling: situations which all make it difficult to shoot line on the next cast, leading to casting struggles and less efficient fishing. It also prevents the line from tangling on vegetation such as lily pads in weedy situations which can be much more annoying than line drag caused by line drifting away or downstream. However, there are some inconveniences, inefficiencies and hassles with storing line on board the kayak. First, it will tangle on almost anything that is physically possible, even the buttons on your shirt. You may even need to take off your watch, when for some improbable reason, Murphy's Law becomes unnaturally fixated upon it. Hatch straps, paddle leashes, and even additional loops of flyline on longer casts can be a problem. However, most of the inconvenience and inefficiency problems are caused by the constricted line stripping motions required to deposit the line in a safe position within the narrow confines of the kayak. Many flyfishing situations, especially in saltwater and especially in a moving kayak, require full extension of the retreiving arm to manage slack line and to successfully retrieve a fly in a manner that will attract and eventually set the hook on a fish. An extra arm motion is required in order to place the line in the kayak after each stripping motion. It doesn't sound like much, but once you've tried it, you will notice that it can drastically change the retrieve on a fly. If the kayak is drifting toward the fly, it can become increasingly difficult and sometimes almost impossible to achieve an effective retrieve.

Bassbugging the pads by kayak

Flatsboats, bassboats, jonboats and even canoes all have plenty of room to throw flyline onto the deck after a full stripping motion. Try this motion in a kayak, and you suddenly realize how confined is your craft. Your line is overboard and possibly tan-

gling in weeds, drifting away in the current or windblown surface. On longer casts, you can have quite a bit of line overboard,
creating line drag or intertwining in the weeds as you drift away.
Casting can sometimes be an exercise in frustration and so inefficient that it becomes difficult to catch fish.

So, what is the solution to become a graceful and efficient
flycaster by kayak? Actually, there are multiple solutions according to the situation, including casting adjustments, immobilizing
the kayak, sitting side saddle, getting out of the kayak, and constructing a floating stripping basket. In varying situations, you
might find one solution more advantageous or convenient than
another.

In situations where it is best to keep the kayak drifting in the
wind, paddling along, or continuously moving, it is helpful if
you can keep the line in the kayak. Keeping your casts shorter
will help prevent line from tangling upon itself in your kayak. A
surface bug or popper is sometimes easier to work in a moving
situation. Do not try to fish in the direction that the kayak is
drifting. The kayak will overtake your fly, and it will be a difficult chore to strip and remove slack line, much less retrieve the
lure. Instead, cast at an angle out to the side of the kayak, and
when the lure begins to drag due to line and fly trailing the kayak,
simply lift the line and recast out to the side again. This is a very
effective technique for searching large areas of water to locate
fish, especially when combined with a *zig-zag drift technique*
(see Chapter 9: *Kayakfishing Skills & Techniques*).

In circumstances where the kayak is immobilized, a flycaster
can strip line over the side of the kayak without experiencing
water drag on the loose coils after retrieving the line. In circumstances where it would be advantageous to make the craft stationary, there is more than one way to stop a kayak. An anchor is
one way, and it is very convenient in shallow water, but it is not
always necessary. Sometimes weedcover and vegetation are thick
enough to slow a kayak's drift or to stop drifting movement. Yet,
a light stroke of the paddle has you moving again. The actual
dynamics and convenience depend upon the thickness of the vegetation and the windspeed. Many fisherman carry a clamping de-

vice on a short cord to quickly clamp onto lily pads, branches or logs where it is not convenient or advisable to throw over an anchor. Oftentimes, the same vegetation that entangled your flyline and made flycasting seem impossible can actually enhance casting performance by serving as a surface on which the line can be laid. The vegetation prevents the line from sinking and spreads the coils allowing improved shooting of the flyline.

Flyrodding for surface feeding stripers

Some kayaks are extremely stabile, especially those that are designed for diving enthusiasts. They were designed for a diver to slip overboard and dive and after returning to the surface, to reboard the kayak. This is good news for all kayakfishermen and especially to flyfishermen because it means that they can sit side saddle on their kayaks without tipping them over. It is an advantage to kayakers, in general, to occasionally change their seating position for the purposes of comfort and for the ability to access otherwise unreachable areas of the kayak. But for a flyfisherman, it means that you can sit in a fully upright positon similar to sitting on the edge of a dock with plenty of room to toss the extra coils of flyline into the seat area with a normal fully extended retrieving stroke. A flyfisherman can utilize this position while drifting or anchored. The only drawback is that you cannot paddle as effectively from this postion, but it is surprisingly safe and stable. It is also probably the best flycasting position from the kayak (see photo on page 72).

However, some of the most enjoyable flyfishing is done by kayak after jumping out to wade. The flyfisherman gets to stand or walk upright, enjoying a backcast that is naturally higher off the water. Also your hands can concentrate fully on flycasting, since your feet handle directional changes and forward motion as you search for fish. During a full day of kayakfishing, it is often a nice change of pace to get out and walk and give yourself a position break. If you have ever waded while flyfishing, you will appreciate using a kayak not only for the efficient transportation to the wading area, but also because of all the extra gear and comfortable amenities that can be towed along by kayak (see Chapter 9: *Kayakfishing Skills & Techniques*). A kayak is much more enjoyable to tow along behind you than a bigger boat while flyfishing for several reasons. It is easier to pull along behind you even with the anchor out. Also, if you want anything from the kayak such as a drink or a bite of your sandwich, one tug on the rope and the bow of the kayak is at your fingertips. Most important to a flyfisher though, your backcast will rarely ever catch on the kayak as it often does while towing along larger craft.

The most effective all around improvement to my kayak flyfishing efforts, however, came about after constructing a floating stripping basket. It can be attached to the kayak by velcro straps so that, when thrown overboard, it is positioned right where your stripping motion would end, depositing the line effortlessly and safely into the confines of the basket. Therefor, it cannot drift away or catch on any weeds no matter how much you drift, how fast the current, or how many weeds you pass through. In addition, the basket can also serve as a landing net, and a live fish holding pen before or after you unhook your fish, particularly if you want a picture before you release the fish. It not only works while casting from the kayak, but it can also be strapped to a wading belt to use while wading. It is made from foam Fun Noodles that kids use to swim and play with in the water. It has a mesh bag attached below and adjustable velcro straps to attach it to the straps on a kayak seat or to a wader's belt (see photos on pages 151 and 153). If you have a cooler mounted behind your backrest, you can place the basket behind the seat to serve as an additional back cushion when not in use.

It doesn't get any better

Kayak flyfishing is a fun and enjoyable experience wherever it is practiced. In the ocean, it can be fantastic just outside the surf for stripers and bluefish, or in the open ocean for a variety of possibilities, and in rivers, it can be both a scenic paddle and productive flyfishing. Large meandering rivers where you can take take your time and place a bug beside a mossy stump can be relaxing to the soul. For excitement, consider rushing downstream in a rocky creek quickly making multiple short cast placements of a high floating dry fly back into pockets of water holding trout that rarely get fished.

Chapter Eleven

Kayak Lure Fishing

Bass caught on a surface *buzzed* plastic worm

Why is artificial lure fishing so good by kayak, and how can you take the best advantage of it? Well, there are a number of reasons why it is so effective. You are always ready to go on short notice with a minimum of hassle. When fish are biting well, you can catch more fish with artificial lures. Kayaks are ideal for active fishermen who are on the move searching, exploring, finding fish, and eliminating unproductive water. Their tackle and lure selections are ready to go when conditions are most opportune. Kayak lure fishermen get to the lake quicker. They do not need to make a stop at the bait shop, and when they get to the lake, they do not mess around with castnets, livewells or keeping live bait alive. They get right down to the business of finding fish, and they are more efficient at doing just that. The kayak-lure combination is a natural for covering water and finding fish. Rather than choosing a spot and waiting while a baitfish attracts a fish, kayak lure fishermen are on the move, fishing many areas and types of water. They put the lures right in there where they want them. They go to the fish. They get into the tough, inaccessible places. They eliminate the bad water, find the good water, fish it hard and move on. Live bait can be very uncooperative and slow, but with lures, you can control the placement, depth, speed, and action of your offering. By understanding the dynamic advantages of kayaks and lures to your fishing, you can emphasize your efforts in the areas where you can make the best of your opportunities. You can maximize the amount of time that your lures are placed in front of actively biting fish.

Artificial fishing lures work best when the fish are active and aggressive. Fish make more mistakes then. They are usually active and aggressive when weather and environmental conditions combine to create favorable feeding periods, and when they are subjected to very little fishing pressure. The requirements vary for different species and for specific environments. Some of the major influential factors to be considered are weather conditions, gravitational forces (moon phases and daily activity periods), tides, water levels, weed levels, food or baitfish levels and reproductive activities. Kayakfishermen tend to get out fishing more often due to the reduced equipment, hassle, expense, and time required. Therefor, they have increased odds of going more often and being there at the right time to experience one of those feeding binges when a number of the positive major influential factors come into alignment. If they develop the experience to predict those feeding binges, they are also more likely to get away to experience it on a regular basis. For a small investment of time and money, their efforts can develop into a consistently fantastic fishing experience.

Inaccessible areas

Kayaks are great for getting into inaccessible areas where fishing pressure is light. Sometimes the fishing pressure is always light as in a remote pond or other permanently difficult to access situation. In other situations, the pressure may be off for a season as in a low water situation or for only a day or even hours as in a tidal or weather situation. When fishing pressure is off whether long term or short term, the odds are relatively higher for fish to strike artificials. The fishing still fluctuates according to environmental and weather conditions, but generally, the fish will be less wary and easier to catch on artificials. A private pond almost always has better bass fishing, and most bass fishermen know that the second time they fish their way down a bank is rarely as good as the first time on any given day or lake. The most impulsive fish are quickly caught. They are the fish that are likely to make a mistake at that point in time.

Remote ponds are a situation that would be inaccessible on a permanent basis. Small, narrow or shallow creeks would be other long term opportunities that might be overlooked by other anglers. Sometimes sections of larger creeks can be difficult to access by most anglers due to fallen trees or rocks obstructing navigation. Some rivers or creeks can be seasonally inaccessible due to low water. Low water can prevent anglers from seasonally or permanently accessing areas on larger lakes. Sometimes there may be deeper water further back, but getting to it is too difficult or time consuming for big boat anglers. If there are rocks, then the threat of propeller damage is often not worth the uncertainty of catching a fish. The temporary low water effects of tides can also present low fishing pressure situations for kayakfishermen. Often hot sections of saltwater shallow flats are unavailable to even the shallowest running boats, especially where there is an abundance of grass, rocks, oyster bars or coral. Many hours of fantastic fishing can often be had before the other boats can get in there to mine the potholes ahead of the tidal inflow. Small tidal creeks often have deep holes in the bends where currents wash away continuously. However, getting to those holes might be impossible at low tide, except by kayak.

Weeds can also create accessibility problems for most anglers. Some lake areas normally have large areas of heavy vegetation that are impenetrable by motorized craft, especially on southern lakes. At times, weed cover gets unusually heavy and expansive for a season. Huge areas may hold many fish that big boats cannot push through without engine damage. Trolling motors often hang up or are too noisy to operate, scaring any fish close enough to catch. Weeds are almost never a problem for fish. They thrive in it. Weeds are also no problem for a kayak. They can create an oasis of private fishing water in the middle of a public lake. Fish buried back in a large expanse of vegetation may not have seen a fishing lure for a long, long time. Odds are that they would respond very favorably on presentation.

Weather can make larger public lakes inaccessible to all but the most foolish traditional boaters, and yet be perfectly safe for a kayaker. Most bigger lakes must be navigated out in the open, deeper water where winds are the most treacherous, but kayaks can travel the safety of the shallows where you can get out and walk if necessary. Of course, you must know your lake and the lake bottom. Some days in the middle of the hottest fishing season, there are no other boats on the water, and the fish are very aggressive in their absence. Lure fishing can be as good as it gets. If many larger boats show up, the fish go back into hiding. Although the main lake may be ugly, the shallows are often relatively calm, especially on the leeward shore. Just be sure you know the weather threat, know your lake, and watch out for lightening.

Stealth

Kayaks give lure fishermen a degree of stealth that is unequaled by any other craft. It is such a low impact entry into an environment that fish are either unaware or unconcerned with its presence. It will rarely affect fish in a manner to put off their feeding or aggressive behavior. You will often find yourself surrounded by a large school of redfish that do not seem to recognize you as a threat; but instead, seem to mill about with some individuals actually hiding beneath your kayak. Schools of tarpon will sometimes allow you to enter their school and paddle among them as they roll on the surface, and then they actually strike your lures. Largemouth bass schooling on shad will sometimes actually bang into your kayak as they excitedly chase their prey across the surface, and sometimes they bang their heads when chasing your lures. These are admittedly unusual examples but, at the same time, exemplary of the stealthy nature of kayaks.

Seatrout caught on a soft plastic jerkbait

Lure fishing techniques

Your fishing technique should maximize your oppurtunity for a strike and should be appropriate for the situation. Unless you have a good idea where the fish are located, you should use a technique that allows you to cover a lot of water until you detect a pattern. Kayaks are great for quietly covering a large area of water, and when combined with a fishing technique that is also effective at covering water, the result is efficiency. The cast, presentation, and retrieve of your lures should be made in such a manner as to avoid spooking the fish that you have so carefully and quietly approached. Fish in shallow fresh or saltwater are especially susceptible to spooking, especially if the water is clear. Water that is off color or water that has vegetation, logs, rocks or other cover that can potentially obscure the fish's view will lessen the odds of spooking the fish. However, those same obstructions of the fish's view will make it more difficult for them to see your lure. So, you may need to help them to locate it by using their sense of sound. The trick is to guage the level of sound to the environmental situation. In shallow water, you may actually see the fish spook, or they may just hold tight in the cover and refuse to strike. So, if you are not getting strikes, you may need to make some adjustments to the disturbance or noise levels that you are using to attract a strike. The adjustments might be a change in the speed or nature of your retrieve or perhaps a change to another fishing lure. One of the most common factors of unusually successful lure fishermen is their ability to detect the need for subtle changes in their presentations and their skill at implimenting them. That is why two guys can be using the exact same lure with totally differing results.

Once you have detected a pattern you may need to move along faster to fish the next piece of similar cover type that is holding the fish, or you may need to slow down in order to concentrate your efforts in an area with a high concentration of fish or cover that is holding fish. You may even want to get out of the kayak and wade in some areas to thoroughly and stealthily cover the area before moving on. However, the area that holds the concentration of fish may not be shallow enough to wade. It may even be deep, and it may not have any cover. The fish may not even be concentrated. The lures and techniques to fish the area will probably change, but the fishing efficiency principal will not. You will still try to cover water quickly to eliminate water, find a concentration of fish, or discover a pattern. Upon detecting a pattern, you will probably alter your efforts to increase your efficiency.

There is a core of standard lure fishing techniques that should be mastered and adapted to your own style of kayak lure fishing, keeping the efficiency principle mentioned previously in mind. At the top of the list, obviously, is topwater fishing. Classic topwater fishing is done with a plug. In order to maximize the advantages of a kayak, an angler searching for fish should use a topwater plug that works well moving along and covering water. Zara Spooks and many of the newer lures that copy its irresistable action are a great choice but require a little experience and concentration to work properly. The plugs with propellors fore and/or aft are easier to work and very effective when fished at any retrieval rate. They are very versatile. You can fish them faster than a Zara Spook or slower than a popper. There are many makes and styles of poppers. There is the classic Hula Popper for bass, and the more versatile minnow imitating style of plug typified by the Rebel Pop-R. One of the advantages of a cup faced popper is that you can keep it in one place longer while attempting to lure a fish that you believe is there watching. Some of the minnow imitating poppers can be fished a little faster, but generally a popper is a better lure for when you have a good idea where the fish are located.

Buzzing

Another form of topwater fishing is ideally suited to searching for fish by kayak. *Buzzing* is a technique that involves the steady retrieval of a surface disturbing lure over the surface to attract fish upward for the strike. The speed of the retrieve and the noise level are adjusted to match the environmental conditions and the mood of the fish. Buzzing is a very popular technique with bass fishermen, especially when the bass are hiding in heavy cover, but the technique is also effective on many species of predatory fish. Lures for buzzing are the classic bass buzzbaits with propellers on a wire shaft, paddle wheel baits such as Bill Norman's Weedwalker, spinnerbaits which are considered to be primarily bass lures but are effective top to bottom for a number of species, soft plastic lures with either curly or paddle tails including both grubs and plastic worms, and a miscellaneous assortment of surface agitating variations of the previously mentioned examples. The soft plastic lures may be the most versatile of all the buzz baits as the degree of surface agitation can be adjusted through tail size and style, and because they are also effectivly fished from top to bottom so that a number of techniques may be incorporated into one retrieve. On a single cast, you can buzz over the surface to attract attention, drop into a pocket in cover, bounce a few times off the bottom, and return to buzzing. One of the great advantages of the soft plastic baits is that—if you miss a strike, the fish are likely to strike it again, and they usually hang on to them longer, allowing you more time to set the hook.

Jerkbaits

Another style of fishing soft plastic baits is called *jerk bait* fishing. Jerk baits typically have a straight form and are usually fished weightless. They most often represent baitfish and can be molded as detailed minnows, but they can represent shrimp, crayfish, or undeterminable but favorable dining oppurtunities. The classic fishing style is an erratic, darting motion of widely varying speeds usually just beneath the surface. But, they can be very effective when skittered across the surface as a panicking baitfish, and especially the minnow imitations can be deadly when allowed to sink with twitching motions that create spasdic, intermittent, random directional movements similar to a dying baitfish. Jerk bait fishing first became popular with bass fishermen in freshwater, but it quickly became a favorite technique for shallow inshore saltwater fishermen.

Skipping

Skipping is a technique that is used to get lures underneath structures or cover over the water surface that fish may be hiding under such as docks or overhanging trees. The low-on-the-water perspective of a kayakfisherman is especially conducive to skipping lures under objects. It is the same concept as a kid skipping stones over the water. This is a deadly technique when cover loving species such as largemouth bass and snook refuse to come out for a strike. However, kayakfishermen should be skilled at paddling backward with one hand while fighting a fish with the rod holding hand. The skipping technique often hooks fish large enough to pull your kayak under the trees or a dock while fighting them on a tight drag. Besides back paddling, there are two other alternatives to being pulled under the dock: quickly tossing out an anchor and wading. Wading is probably the most efficient way to fight fish that are holding back under obstructions. If the bottom is solid and shallow enough, you should hop out and wade once you've located an area with a concentration of fish. But if you are skilled at back paddling with one hand, it would be better to search for a productive area first by kayak because you can cover more water. Many lure types are often used for skipping, but weightless soft plastic jerkbaits are probably the best because of their even weight distribution. The minnow shaped baits are the best skippers due to their flatter shape. Their spasdic random sideways movements tend to keep them under the cover longer than more cyllindrical shaped lures.

Cranking

Cranking is typically done with sinking or floating/diving plugs. By selecting the appropriate plug, a fisherman can control the speed and depth of the lure by adjusting the retrieve and the line weight. Crankbaits are very effective when you know the depth where fish are holding. They are also effective when you do not know where the fish are located because they cover a lot of water quickly, especially when trolled. When used in conjunction with a depthfinder or fishfinder they can be deadly. Their biggest drawback is that they typically have treble hooks which hang up easily on any vegetation below or floating loose on the surface. Cranking can also be accomplished with some styles of jigs which tend to be much more weedless.

Jigging

Jigs are probably the most versatile and effective lures. Of course, they come in a wide array of weights and styles. They can be fished at any depth or speed, and they can be adapted to almost any of the standard fishing techniques, including topwater buzzing, jerk baiting, skipping, mid-depth cranking, flipping, finesse fishing, standard jig bottom bouncing, and trolling. Jigs can even be fished in combination with live or cut bait. One of the little known and used techniques with high performance results is the jig and bobber combination. It is commonly used for pulling crappie from sunken branches and treetops. It is also used very effectively on saltwater flats to catch seatrout hiding in eelgrass. The slender torpedo shaped bobber swished over the surface sounds like a baitfish and attracts the trout that are hiding in the eelgrass. The trout then easily find a soft plastic jig that hovers just over the eelgrass. The technique is also deadly for many other species of fish found on the saltwater flats, especially redfish. The technique also works very well while trolling the rig behind the kayak. Your paddling can be adjusted to enhance the action of the jig and bobber rig behind the kayak.

Flipping

Flipping is a technique for fishing in heavy cover such as weeds, logs, branches or brush. It is especially effective on largemouth bass, but it is often used for crappie, bluegill and other panfish. Standard casting and retrieving will not allow you to get a lure down deep under the cover and then to retrieve it back without hanging up in the cover. A more vertical approach allows you to drop your lure into small openings in the cover and allows it to fall naturally, and hopefully, right on the nose of a willing fish. Flipping allows an angler to place a lure in front of a fish without making a loud splash as the lure enters the water. A kayak is perfect for flipping because it easily penetrates very heavy weeds quietly without spooking the fish. Flipping is usually done with either a soft plastic lure rigged *Texas style* with a pegged slip sinker or with a weedless jig and a skirt with a trailer of either soft plastic or pork rind. The pork rind trailer chosen most often is the flatter frog style. This trailer allows the jig to sink more slowly, giving the fish more time to react since they usually hit on the drop. It also gives the angler more time to react because the pork rind has a meaty lifelike feel that causes the bass to hold on longer. Although a slow fall is important, sometimes you need more weight to break through some of the thicker weeded areas. Heavy rods and line are required because you will need to muscle the fish out of weeds, brush, or logs on a short line without a drag. It is one of the most deadly tactics on the bass fishing tournament trail and has probably won more tournaments than any other single technique. The rods that are designed for flipping, however, typically have longer handles. The extra long handles can be a nuisance due to the sitting position in the kayak. Any longer rod with a not-so-long handle can be substituted for the traditonal flipping stick. The handles of conventional flipping sticks can also be shortened to accomadate their use in the kayak.

Finesse fishing

Finesse fishing is a style of fishing that typically involves the use of light line and smaller lightweight lures. This style of fishing is usually practiced in less weedy water, but not necessarily. The light line and small lures are used to encourage non agressive, high pressured, or simply difficult fish to take the lure. It is a common style of fishing in shallow or clear water and on heavily fished lakes. It is also popular for inshore saltwater flatsfishing, especially in the skinny water. It is usually an intense form of fishing in which the angler knows precisely where he, at least, thinks the fish are located and concentrates his efforts there. Often the fish are visible and the technique can be a form of *sightfishing*. The lures used can be anything from tiny topwater lures, crankbaits, or more commonly, soft plastics often in combination with small lightweight jigheads. Although finesse fishing often utilizes light to ultra light tackle, very large fish are often hooked. Light tackle fish fighting skills and regular tackle maintenance are required. Kayaks are particularly well suited to finesse fish due to their superior stealth advantage.

Trolling

Trolling has some special advantages in general, and it has some strategic benefits in particular to kayakfishermen. In some fishing situations you may not know where the fish are located. There may be no attracting structure, cover, currents, or bait schools. There may be much water to cover. It is a tough scenario but a common one that often holds many fish. Most successful conventional boat anglers resort to trolling and most often with the help of a fishfinder to find the depth of the fish. Some kayakfishermen are opposed to a depthfinder for a variety of reasons, but trolling is very popular. It raises a kayaker's odds of catching fish in open water when they do not know where the fish are located, but more than that, it may be the only feasible way to fish when traveling upwind in very windy conditions when your hands are fully occupied with the paddle. It is also a great way to pick up some bonus fish when traveling to and from targeted fishing areas. It is also a great way to fish some live bait out the back while you are busy casting lures up front. You can reap the compounded benefits of trolling, casting, live bait and lures. For many kayakfishermen, trolling is just a great way to get out for a paddle, to relax, and to catch a few fish along the way.

Key to Success

The key to success is knowing your fish and their environment, having a good fishing plan, selecting and fishing the right lures, tackle, and techniques. Then you need to learn from experience and make adjustments to your plan. Daily and long term. Always keep in mind your advantages and disadvantages of fishing by kayak. Some species of fish will bite better in different weather and environmental circumstances than others. If you are a single species aficionado, you had best know the environmental and weather conditions for your outing and how your target species might react under those circumstances. This knowledge can make the difference in knowing which lures, tackle and techniques you will need, and where in the environment to apply them. It may even tip you off to put your outing on hold for that particular day and wait a few days when conditions may improve. However, bad conditions for one species are often just the ticket for another. Multiple species targets are a good hedge.

Caught on a slider worm on top of lily pads to imitate dragonflies

A good example in freshwater would be the largemouth bass with an impending cold front. On cold fronts, largemouth bass lose a great deal of their aggression. They tend to hide deep in cover and usually will not venture far to attack prey. Techniques and lures that produced outstanding results a day earlier on a warm front can get you skunked a day later on a cold front. A kayak bass fisherman has a few options in such a situation. He can stay home a few more days until a warmfront returns, adjust his lure fishing techniques, switch to live bait which tends to work better than lures on coldfronts, or switch to another cold front loving species such as trout, pickerel or pike. The hardcore artificial lure bass fisherman who understands the nature of large-mouth bass during coldfronts would switch to a technique such as flipping. When flipping, a bass fishermen gets a very weedless lure into the heavy cover where they are hiding and attempts to quietly place a sinking lure right on the bass's nose, hoping for an impulsive strike reaction. It is an extremely specialized and effective technique (see Flipping previously covered in this chapter).

Chapter Twelve

Kayak Live Bait Fishing

Larry Timmerman with a big bass and golden shiner

It is not surprising that some kayakfishermen are diehard livebait fishermen. Far more trophy fish are caught on live bait in freshwater, and in saltwater, you may hook something bigger than your kayak. Live bait catches bigger fish, and when the fish are not aggressively feeding, sometimes it is the only way to catch them. It is not always the fastest or most productive, but it is very consistent. Live bait fishermen do not get skunked as often as artificial lure fishermen. But there are other reasons to fish live bait. Some fishermen like to watch the drama of the chase when a big fish traps a baitfish against the surface and then the *blow up* as the predator makes a move to inhale the bait. Sometimes there are multiple blow ups if the baitfish is particularly elusive or if the bigger fish wants to play with it, as they often do. Sometimes after all the savagery, the predator simply disappears without taking the bait. So, there is often a drama played out before the gratifying realization that something big has your bait and is peeling line off your reel just before you take a shot at setting the hook. Aside from the productivity and excitement of fishing live bait, some fishermen like to fish live bait because it can be more relaxing. At least, until the predator finds the prey. Livebait, however, does not always mean baitfish. Other creatures such as shrimp, crabs, crayfish, helgrammites, clams, bloodworms and earthworms can put a lot of fish in the kayak. There are many ways to fish and rig your live bait. You can learn to catch your own bait or in many cases buy it commercially, but you will have to know how to keep it alive which can be relatively easy or difficult depending on what bait you need for your target species. There are some advantages to fishing live bait from a kayak, especially if you are fortunate enough to hook a big fish. There can be some challenges, however, to actually landing a very big fish.

Live baitfish

Baitfish are the most exciting to fish from a kayak. Live baitfish give kayak anglers the chance to catch some truly outsized fish of many species. You can fish them on the surface under floats, tight line them, weight them, or fish them on jigs. You can troll them, drift them, stillfish, cover coax, or flip them into heavy cover. Live baitfish can be used as fishfinders, and they will inform you of a predator's presence. Even if the gamefish does not eat or even threaten your baitfish, it will probably panic at the sight of a bigger fish in the area. You will often feel the sudden increase in frantic movement through your rod and fishing line.

Fish are not always ready to feed, but if you know the fish is there, you can concentrate your efforts in the area or move on for awhile and return later. When a bigger gamefish gets serious about your baitfish, the big fish will approach from below, often driving your bait to the surface. The baitfish will struggle at the surface and often jump into the air in an attempt to escape.

Trolling

You can troll your baitfish with a float to keep it near the surface, or you can tightline it. *Tightlining* is done with no float and no weight so that the baitfish swims unhindered and natural. A float keeps the bait near the surface and also helps to attract gamefish. A baitfish at the surface is more noticeable, vulnerable, and tempting to predators. The float often adds additional attractive power to get your bait noticed. However, gamefish are occasionally float shy, and tightlining can get you strikes when floats are spooking off your fish. Sometimes tightlining allows a baitfish to hang up on bottom or in weeds, especially when paddling very slow or in shallow water. A float will allow you to troll very slowly and even stop in an area that may be holding fish. If you use *slotted* floats with removable pegs, then you can add a float in seconds or remove it without cutting off the hook or removing your baitfish. If a big fish repeatedly blows up on your bait but refuses to take it, you will appreciate the slotted float feature when you pitch the bait back to the fish without the float only seconds later, and he eats it. Trolling baitfish behind your kayak requires a good solid rodholder to prevent the loss of your rod. However you can set your reel on freespool with just enough drag to prevent the spool from overspinning your line into a snarl as the fish heads away with your bait. Then you can pick up the rod and engage the gears to set the hook. With a sturdy rodholder, you can keep paddling with the reel in gear and a tight drag, letting the kayak's forward motion set the hook. Circle hooks work very effectively for this purpose. Paddling forward is a great way to search for fish, but paddling backwards allows you to watch the baitfish for any nervous behavior and gives you a great view of some awsome strikes. Hook the baitfish in the mouth and out the nostril.

Drifting

Drifting with live baitfish also has the advantages of covering much water and utilizing the nervous behavior of baitfish as a gamefish *presence indicator*. It is a good idea to carry a few markers to throw when observing frantic behavior in open water areas. This technique works effectively when used in combination with trolling and stillfishing. When you mark an area while drifting downwind, you can troll by it again heading upwind. If no strike occurs, you may want to drop anchor and stillfish the area on your next drift downwind. When drifting or stillfishing, your hands are not occupied with the paddle. If your kayak has a stable design that will allow it, you can sit side saddle. You can also put out an extra rod. On one rod you can use a float and tightline with the other rod. If you are drifting too fast, you can put out a sea anchor which acts similar to a parachute to slow your drift. You can put out more than one. If you need more help to slow down, you can set out your anchor temporarily or come to a full stop to still fish.

Still fishing

Still fishing works best when you know where the fish are located. Still fishing gives the baitfish a chance to work on triggering a predator's instinctive responses to attack. Sometimes they attack immediately, but other times you may have to wait for a feeding or *activity period* to occur in order to raise your odds for a strike to occur. Most often it is best to hook the baitfish on the back (dorsal side), unless you will be still fishing in combination with drifting and trolling. Cast the the baitfish away from your kayak and begin to coax it further away from your kayak by adding a little resistance to the line. The natural response of the baitfish is to struggle against the resistance much like a dog straining on a leash. Give it a little slack to encourage it along. As the baitfish begins to tire, it will eventually return closer to the kayak. You can recast, but repeated casting further saps their strength. If you use a float, it will allow the baitfish to hang upright until it catches its breath rather than sinking to the bottom. A light tug at the float occasionally will help to attract a fish and keep the baitfish advertising for a strike. At times, it is more effective to stillfish in combination with trolling and drifting. You will need to hook the baitfish in the mouth and out the nostril. Troll it behind the kayak until it is in the target area. Then when the baitfish returns to the kayak, paddle a circular path that repositions the baitfish back in the target area. You can then drop anchor or hold position with your paddle.

Cover coaxing

Cover coaxing is usually done while still fishing, but it can be done on the move. It is commonly used to catch largemouth bass on shiners, but it can be adapted for use on other species hiding in cover. After a gentle cast, you want the baitfish to swim away from you and preferably into or underneath some form of cover or at least up against it. *Cover* is something the fish use to hide in or under. It is usually surface covering or emerging aquatic vegetation, flooded terrestrial vegetation, log jams, undercut banks, docks, pilings, or moored boats et cetera. By hooking the baitfish in the back, you can pull backward on it. As the baitfish instinctively fights to escape, you feed slack allowing it to charge back under the cover. Hooking the baitfish in the back also allows it to hang on the hook in an upright position below a float when it becomes tired. Going floatless, however, will allow the baitfish to get further back under surface vegetation because a float often hangs up, preventing a baitfish from forcing its way deeper into the vegetation. Hooking the baitfish over the anal fin is a technique often used to swim a baitfish far back under heavy weedcover. It only works well with a lively baitfish. Tired baitfish will sink. Using a float will only cause a weary baitfish hooked in this manner to hang upside down. However, a hook placed in the anal fin area will tear out easily, allowing for a good hookset.

A weedless hook should be used when fishing around cover. You should use a heavy rod and fishing line of about 30 lb. test because you will need to horse fish away from the heavy cover. Cover coaxing is very taxing on the baitfish, so you will need a good supply. You will go through bait much quicker than with most other techniques except flipping.

Flipping

Flipping is a popular technique that is used to catch large-mouth bass on artificials, and sometimes panfish such as bluegill and crappie. However, sometimes anglers will use heavy poles and line to flip large golden shiners into pockets in heavy cover such as hydrilla, floating hyacinths or into a dense concentration of lily pads to haul out some humungous bass. For the panfish, a tiny jig tipped with small minnows is lowered into the aquatic jungle. When flipping, you do not cast. You use a rod length of line to swing your bait to the target with a pendulum-like motion. The idea is to get a quiet entry into the water as close to the fish as possible. A kayak is ideal for flipping baitfish because you can penetrate the heavy weeds so quietly without spooking the fish, slip right up and set the bait on their nose. While flipping large baitfish such as shiners, you not only feel the line for signs of your baitfish panicking but also watch the the surrounding weeds for signs of movement. Usually you will see the weeds shake when the baitfish panicks at the approach of a big bass, and often you will see weeds parting or lily pads knocking as a bass charges up to investigate. The technique also works well for pulling snook out from under mangroves, boats and docks. You need a long rod stiff rod, heavy line, and a tight drag to wrestle big fish into the kayak in a close up battle.

Popular baitfish

Huge largemouth bass are caught every day on *golden shiners* in the state of Florida, especially in the winter months. They are the number one trophy bass producer. Many large bass are caught on them in other states as well. However, in Florida they are widely sold commercially. The reason is simple. Bass prefer them over any other food. In other states, they are not so widely available commercially, but they are always in great demand by the bass wherever they swim. You can easily catch your own.You can use hog feed or soybean meal to attract them to an area and then either castnet them or use white bread on tiny hooks to catch them. You will need a good live bait tank. Shiners, especially large shiners, are very effective as a fishfinder. Shiners are very hypertensive creatures, and they have a very low panic threshold. And for good reason. They have about as much of a chance of going unmolested during a day as an icecream sundae has of

Golden shiners are the best bait for big largemouth bass

melting away uneaten in a room full of kids. Trolling them is the best way to find bass if you do not already know where they will be hiding. Even if you do not get a strike, mark the places where the shiner telegraphed its fear. After a time, turn around and re-test the areas, eventually your trolling areas get smaller and smaller. When repeated passes over the same area give the same responses from the shiner, you know the bass are there. You may even drop the anchor, it's only a matter of time. Often that time is the first time your shiner passes by the bass. Cover coaxing and flipping can also produce awsome results when you know where bass are located in heavy cover. About the best chance a shiner has of not being eaten by a bass is that some other predator will eat it first. All predatory fish in fresh or saltwater will eat and enjoy shiners. They are great bait for musky, pike, pickerel, small-mouth bass, striped bass, walleye, crappie, tarpon, cobia, snook, redfish, and flounder et cetera.

Mullet

Mullet are exciting to fish because of the way they jump away from gamefish. Even when hooked on a line, they sometimes elude their pursuers. They are probably the most common forage fish in saltwater, but they are also common in freshwater. Unfor-tunately for them everywhere they are found, all the predators would like to eat them. They are often seen jumping repeatedly when not being chased. You can tell they are not being chased by the way they jump. Lazy jumps followed by loud belly flops seem to be just for fun. People often ask why they spend so much of their days making those pointless jumps. It's probably because they are so tasty: they have to stay in shape to stay one jump ahead of the gamefish. That is just what they do as they speedily fly over the surface like flying fish barely touching the water. No belly flops. Put a hook and line on one to slow him down, and he becomes irressistible to all saltwater gamefish. In freshwater, largemouth bass, pickerel, and striped bass will take advantage of an oppurtunity to dine on them, especially the fingerlings.

The most exciting way to fish mullet is on the surface with a float. Trapped on the surface, it presents an enticing target. How-ever, the mullet's jumping abilities often frustrate a predator even with the drag from the float attached. They are sometimes able to escape even on the end of your line. Using a tightline without the float, the sinking line puts a downward strain on the mullet. Al-though it will struggle to the surface, it is difficult for them to jump. They also tire more quickly. Tired mullet are easier to catch and easier to catch fish on. Mullet are also very effective when fished on the bottom with or without weights. You can troll them, drift, or stillfish, especially when anchored near channels with good current. Although larger mullet are often caught on doughballs or small gold hooks at times, most mullet are caught by castnet. In particular, the highly prized fingerling mullet are almost always castnetted. In some areas, live mullet can be bought commercially. Mullet can be kept in an aerated livewell for extended periods as long as they are not overcrowded. They can also be kept alive in the flooded footwells of self bailing sit-on-top kayaks. The constant interchange of water through the scupper holes provides enough oxygen. It helps to place a small wet towel over them to keep them from hopping overboard.

Shad

Shad are probably the most commonly eaten baitfish in freshwater, and some of these species of herring also inhabit saltwater but make spawning runs up into freshwater. Gizzard shad often overpopulate freshwaters and commonly grow to eighteen inches. Since that is rather large for a baitfish, fisheries managers prefer threadfin shad which grow to about 8-10 inches. In large lakes where the gizzard shad population is out of control, fisheries managers have stocked landlocked striped bass with great success. Hickory shad, which grow to about 14 inches, are anadromous and make spawning runs from the ocean up into freshwater rivers. American shad females laden with roe often reach weights of seven pounds or more. They also make the spawning run. All of the shad are readily eaten by all gamefish in fresh and saltwater, especially the juveniles. They travel in large schools and are often attacked by large numbers of gamefish for extended periods in a feeding frenzy often on the surface where the resulting commotion is visible from a distance. This commotion often attracts many birds such as gulls and terns. It should also attract you too. If you do not spot the splashes, make sure you paddle to the birds to check them out. Largemouth bass will sometimes spit out their favorite food, golden shiners, when feeding on shad if they mistakenly inhale a shiner during the excitement. Shad might actually be their true favorite. Striped bass are sometimes almost impossible to catch on artificial lures when there are many shad present. They feed greedily and obviously on the shad, however, often frustrating lure anglers.

Shad are weak swimmers, and do not swim well on a hook and line. They also have very little stamina. They do not live very long at the end of your line. Fortunately, they are usually eaten very quickly when in the proximity of any feeding gamefish. Many anglers will throw some crippled shad overboard around suspended schools of gamefish to spark a feeding frenzy. Usually they have plenty to spare, since they are very easy to spot on the surface of calm water and then throw a castnet over, but they are very difficult to keep alive in a bait tank even when aerated. A circular bait tank helps because they must swim continuously and often get trapped in the corners of square or rectangular livewells. Even in a circular bait tank some begin to die immediately. You may hang onto some lively individuals for a few hours. Throw the weaker individuals over as chum. Some very specialized live bait tanks with extra filtration and aeration have been developed to keep them alive overnight.

Eels

Eels are well known and highly prized as a bait for striped bass. However, they are eaten by many gamefish in both fresh and saltwater. A former Florida state record largemouth bass over 19 pounds was caught on a live eel. The little elvers that somehow make their way from Bermuda all the way to a tiny farm pond in middle America are particularly vulnerable. Large crappie will sometimes have their bellies stuffed with 2-3 inch juvenile eels. The young eels often gather in great numbers below dam spillways while making their way upstream. They are especially vulnerable then. They are capable of crawling overland for hours at a time which makes them particularly suitable for fishing from a kayak because they are easy to keep alive. You can keep them in a mesh bag. Keep them wet and place a wet towel over them. Use the towel to grab them as they are very slippery and likely to escape. Put the hook in the mouth and out through the head, being careful not to puncture the brain. They are best fished tightlined, but they can be fished on a float or with a weight on bottom. They do not troll well as they tend to struggle and wind around the line. An easy and effective way to fish them is as a trailer on a bucktail jig. Eels can be caught in spillways at night with a net and light, in traps with bait, on hook and line with worms as bait, and they can be purchased in many local bait shops.

Choosing baitfish

The best live baitfish for you to fish from your kayak depends upon what area you are from. In the great north in the U.S. and Canada it might be suckers for northern pike or muskellunge. In the northeastern U.S. it might be smelt or menhaden for salmon, bluefish or striped bass. In mid Atlantic states, saltwater anglers use spotfish for weakfish and bluefish when they can get them. In southeastern states and the Gulf of Mexico, many anglers use pinfish which are reminicient of freshwater bluegills. They are extremely spiny, but that does not stop every saltwater gamefish from putting it at the top of their menu wish list. Tarpon, redfish, seatrout, cobia and others all gobble them up. California surf launchers like to use anchovies and mackerel, and they target kelp bass, tuna and thresher sharks. Many different species of killifish and minnows are used just about everywhere.

Tackle

The tackle used for fishing live baitfish varies from one gamefish to another as do the methods used to catch them. However, 20 lb. test line is fine for most big fish, including big sharks and tarpon. Extra line capacity is more important than line weight. It is very difficult to break 20 lb. test in a kayak. The kayak's ability to be towed around easily by a big fish acts as a backup drag system. It is ironic to use 20 lb. test on fish over 100 lbs., and then to use 30 lb. test line for largemouth bass. It is ironic, but wise, trophy bass are capable of breaking 20 lb. test, and they often do, especially in heavy cover. Largemouth bass are very powerful for short distances. Add the fact that they require a powerful hookset, and you have a prescription for a break off. The same style of bass rod known as a *flipping stick* also makes a great live bait rod, not only for bass, but also for those tarpon and sharks in saltwater. They have enough lifting power to move big fish up to the surface at the end of the fight. Baitcasting reels work better than spinning reels with heavy line weights of 20 lb. test or more. A Garcia Ambassadeur 6500 is about right for matching with a flipping stick in most live baitfish situations. *Circle hooks* work fine for most live baitfish. Fish usually hook themselves as they swim away with the bait on a tight line. *Kahle hooks* also work very well, especially when you are trolling.

For many saltwater fish, a shock tippet should be used. Shock tippets help to prevent break offs due to abrasive wear from rough or sharp areas on scales, tails, fin bases, teeth and gill covers. Shock tippets can be connected to your fishing line by a standard leader loop, but lighter fishing line should be doubled over before tying to the leader loop. A *spider hitch* works fine for this purpose. A better connection for your fishing line to the shock tippet is an *Albright Special* which will flow through the guides easier. For large tarpon shock tippets of 80 lb. test should be used. For snook and small tarpon use 30-60 lb.test. For smaller snook to ladyfish and general fishing purposes, a 30 lb. shock tippet is helpful. Even if the fish you are targeting do not have rough, abrasive or sharp areas, the shock tippet will allow you to get a fish under control beside your kayak at the end of a fight. You can grab the line without fear of a line break.

If the fish you are catching are sharp toothed critters such as pickerel, pike, and muskellunge in freshwater or spanish mackerel, barracuda and sharks in saltwater, you should use wire leaders to prevent a cut off. For pickerel and pike with light tackle, you can get by with 10 lb. test leaders, but for bigger pike and muskies 25-30 lb. test would be safer. For sawtoothed spanish mackerel or barracuda stay with the 30 lb. test wire leaders. If large sharks of six foot in length or more are your target use 80 lb. test wire. Messing with sharks large enough to require more than an 80 lb. test wire leader is not a good recommendation. In fact, even small sharks are dangerous to deal with in a kayak (see Chapter 14: *Kayak Fish Handling* and Chapter 15: *Kayakfishing Safety*).

Adding a Live bait tank

The easiest way to add a bait tank to a kayak is to buy a kayak that has an area designed to put a cooler onboard. Usually they are just behind the seat. Coolers have been used successfully on conventional fishing boats for years as bait tanks. You want the cooler to be within easy reach so that you can access your bait as needed. Some kayaks are very stabile and allow you to move around more freely without threat of tipping it over. Nevertheless, you want your bait as close as possible.

To add aeration to the livewell water, you can use either a water recirculating system or an airstone system. A recirculating system uses a bilge pump type motor to pump water up into a PVC pipe with an end cap. A few holes are drilled in the PVC pipe to allow the water to be forced through the holes under pressure, creating agitation at the surface, driving air into the water, mixing it, and recirculating the water to provide dissolved oxygen for the bait. Ready made outfits are sold commercially, but it is easy to construct your own. One of the advantages of a recirculating system is that it can also be used to fill or drain the bait tank. After a few hours, some baitfish tend to pollute the water when they are overcrowded. With a recirculating aerator, it is a simple matter to drain down the water by holding the hose overboard. Then the pump can be placed overboard to pump fresh water into the bait tank. Bilge pumps use 12 volt batteries, but to save on weight you can get a small lawnmower battery or go to a specialty battery shop to find some very small 12 volt batteries.

Airstone aerators use air pumped through a hose and through a porous stone to infuse air bubbles at the bottom of the bait tank to provide dissolved oxygen. One of the advantages of airstone aerators is that many of them operate on one or two flashlite batteries. Some models even have transformers that allow conversion to 12 volts while driving your car or a bigger boat and can even be used with household current when at home. Some even come with rechargeable batteries.

Oxygen infusors are a newer hybrid that uses a bilge pump to suck air into the propeller from an air tube and scatters it in fine bubbles that are blown throughout the tank by the pump. They come in models that sink and models that float on the surface.

One of the most efficient, quiet and hassle free ways to provide oxygen for your bait comes from a company named Oxygenation Systems of Texas. They have a product called The Oxygen Edge that charges your livewell with pure oxygen without the hassle of batteries or electricity. It is also much quieter than other aeration systems.

Many kayaks do not have a space built in for a cooler but do have a hatch just behind the seat. Some kayakfishermen place a five gallon bucket in the hatch opening for a bait container. Then they custom cut the hatch cover to match the circumference of the bucket. In that manner they can avoid cutting into their kayak hull to add a bait tank. Get a bucket with a lid to prevent the tank water from spilling out. Some of the commercially sold aerators are designed for use with a five gallon bucket. Of course, you can cut into any kayak to customize an area to accept a bait tank. Kayak dealers have plastic soldering heat guns for making repairs, and some of them are skilled at customizing kayaks to accept trolling motors, 12 volt batteries, and even glass bottoms for watching the fish below. Be sure you check with a knowledgeable dealer before you start cutting into your kayak and causing irreversible damage to your particular model.

Remember that some types of baitfish require an oval or circular bait tank to continue swimming and strain out enough oxygen to survive. Since they only swim forward, they can get stuck in a corner and die. Shad and other herring commonly present this problem for livebait fishermen. A bucket, rather than a cooler, would work better for them. There are many commercially designed bait tanks on the market of various sizes that are designed more oval or rounded on the ends for this purpose. Fishing catalogues such as Bass Pro Shops carry a wide range of aeration systems and live wells that may work well for you, your particular bait keeping needs, and your model of kayak.

Aquatic Ecosystems is a professional aquaculture supply house that has a large catalogue that can present you with many bait keeping alternatives. In addition to a wide variety of bait tanks, aerators, rechargeable batteries, and nets of every description, they also carry a line of bait tank chemical additive products that you may want to consider. The chemical additive products can be added to your livewell to keep your bait and your catch alive. In many cases, the fish that spend some time in your livewell may actually be healthier than before they went into it. Baitfish often have more stamina after spending a few hours in the chemically treated water which makes them a better bait at the end of your line. Gamefish spending a short time in the treated water have a better chance of survival after release. The products are Bait Holding Formula, Pogey Saver, Finer Shiner, Shrimp Keeper, Please Release Me and Tranquil, and they add electrolytes, dechlorinators, tranquilizers, slime stimulators, bacteria killers and anti fungal agents to your bait tank. You can find the phone number, address and contact information for them and other baitkeeping products companies in the *Kayakfishing Resources* section of this book.

Trolling Bucket

You can keep a few large baitfish alive in a trolling bucket for long periods, but baitbuckets do create a drag behind your kayak while paddling. If you want to paddle faster to a new location, you may need to lift the baitbucket into the kayak. The volume of water available to the baitfish will be reduced and will become stale and low on dissolved oxygen in a short time. You may need to stop periodically to give it a fresh dunking overboard occasionally. Trolling buckets are convenient when you can catch your bait on the water. They are not much help in keeping your bait alive while traveling over land however. Some baitshops shoot oxygen from storage tanks into plastic bags full of bait and water when they sell them to cutomers. Bags full of large shiners can be kept alive for several hours in this manner allowing the customer to reach their fishing destination before releasing the bait into a baitwell or trolling bucket. This technique eliminates the need for an aerated livewell to transport the baitfish over land.

Most of your livebaits, other than live baitfish, are much easier to keep alive in your kayak, and some can be captured right at the fishing scene and used fresh. Shrimp might well be the most widely eaten food item by fish in general. It probably is also the most commonly used bait. They are widely available in baitshops near coastal areas from Virginia south and throughout the Gulf of Mexico. White, brown and pink shrimp are used. You can catch your own at night under a light. The light attracts them, and then you can either dip net them or use a cast net. Of course, your net must have a fine enough mesh to prevent their escape. The really great advantage of shrimp as bait to kayakfishermen might be how easy they are to keep as bait. You can keep them swimming in your aerated livewell, but you can also keep them just as well in your ice cooled cooler in an open plastic bag so that they get some air. They do not need to be kept submerged in water. In fact, if the water is unaerated or too warm, they will die very quickly. You also do not want them in direct contact with the ice in your cooler. The freezing ice will kill them. It is better to set a bit of newspaper over the ice to prevent direct contact.

With shrimp on your hook, you can catch almost anything but plankton and algae eaters. Fresh and saltwater fish have them on their menu wish list. Given the oppurtunity, catfish, bluegill, and bass will all gobble them up. In saltwater, you can catch anything up to jumbo sharks. Huge gator seatrout and redfish are caught by *live-lining* shrimp under mangroves. Trophy snook fishermen like nothing better than a jumbo-sized shrimp as an offering when they can get them, and you will never see a snook or tarpon swim past one.

Fishing with shrimp is about as versatile as it gets. They are fished top to bottom on every type of tackle imaginable. They are fished under many types of floats, including popping corks which are used to attract fish to the shrimp. They are live-lined up under mangroves, docks or other cover. They are fished on the bottom with weight, and they are fished on jigs to bounce a-long the bottom. Some bass fishermen in brackish water creeks use long cane poles to flip juicey shrimp back under docks and into pockets along shoreline cover. They have some phenomenal results with the bass. Most amazing, however, is when a six foot long shark gobbles up a small jig on the bottom because it had a tiny fingernail size piece of shrimp teaser on the artificial lure. Often, just enough to detect the odor is all that is needed.

Grass shrimp

Size is not always a factor as proven by the appeal of tiny grass shrimp. Grass shrimp are usually only about an inch long or less. They are most often used with great success in freshwa-ter for crappie, bluegill, and catfish, but some striped bass fisher-men catch some sizeable fish on the tiny baits. The trick they use is chumming. They intermittently toss a few grass shrimp into the current alongside some undercut sod banks in brackish water creeks where stripers feed on grass shrimp. The unsuspecting stripers follow the free food chain right to their hook. For panfish, grass shrimp are usually fished on a small hook and allowed to sink naturally down to the fish hiding in vegetation. They are also fished on tiny crappie jigs which sometimes help to get them to sink through light vegetation to the fish waiting below. They are very productive fished either way which is why they are car-ried very commonly in many freshwater baitshops. Long cane poles are often used because they allow you to reach out over matted vegetation and drop the shrimp into tiny open pockets. You can catch your own grass shrimp very easily by scooping through shallow water vegetation with a fine mesh net.

They can be kept in an open plastic bag in a cooler or in an aerated livewell, but an airstone aerator is preferred because a recirculating pump is a bit too rough for these delicate crusta-ceans. You could keep them in a small bucket of water in your sit-on-bottom kayak if you change the water occasionally. In a sit-on-top kayak, if you have a smaller sized mesh net available in your kayak, you can scoop up some shrimp and then set the net full of shrimp in the flooded footwells. Then you can use the shrimp directly from the net until they are depleted and then go get another scoop. Kayaks are hard to beat for canepoling little pockets in vegetation with grass shrimp because they can get you back into the right types of areas so effortlessly. You can fish a lot of the right kind of stuff very efficiently.

There are other forms of live bait that are easy to catch and keep while you are on the water. Bait does not come any easier to catch or keep than clams. Many fish in fresh and saltwater gobble them up. In freshwater, you can find mussels that will catch a lot of shellcrackers and catfish. In saltwater, while paddling over shallow flats you can reach down and pull up clams and throw them into your kayak. If you come across some tailing redfish or black drum rooting around the bottom on a shallow flat, you have an ideal scent enhanced fresh bait to toss in their path. It will be easy to find and greedily accepted. Tailing redfish are often difficult to catch on artificial lures because they are so preoccuppied with grubbing around in the sediment with their sense of smell to locate a few sluggish but tasty tidbits. They are often not interested in chasing down elusive prey items.

Crabs are also easy to come by on saltwater flats, especially if you carry a net to scoop them up with. They live very well out of the water, and you can throw them in the kayak with you. If you have a self bailing, sit-on-top kayak with a little water in the footwells, the crab will be happy all day long until you spot that redfish. Just make sure you break his pinchers off or you may not be so happy with him. Crabs, especially blue claw crabs, are also great bait for black drum, tarpon, permit, sheepshead and many others.

Other popular baits are just as easy to keep alive in a kayak and can be bought commercially. Bloodworms are extremely effective on large striped bass but are much more convenient, easier to buy, and easier to keep alive than live baitfish. Earthworms, which can be dug up or bought just about anywhere, are easy to take along and will catch almost everything that swims in freshwater. It is not well known that they will also catch a lot of saltwater fish too. They are especially effective on sheepshead. Stream fishermen use a lot of worms for trout, but they sometimes offer the fish such exquisite cuisine as crayfish or hellgrammites. They catch some dandy smallmouth bass for their efforts. Just about any live bait can be fished effectively by kayak and in most cases, more effectively.

Live bait in its many forms often catches the fish that do not make mistakes. The smarter fish. The bigger fish. When fishing out of a kayak, you will always have the advantage of stealth. Stealth will always be an advantage, but especially so in shallows and in weedy areas. You will also have the advantage of a small, low profile craft that is less intimidating to the fish. You will be able to penetrate weed infested areas easily and efficiently. You will also be able to get into areas that are inaccessable due to rocks, logs, weeds, shallows or remoteness. With all of the advantages to fishing live bait from a kayak, it is inevitable that you will hook some huge fish. Although there are some challenges involved with actually landing huge fish in your kayak, there are some distinct advantages to fighting a big fish from your kayak.

Chapter Thirteen

Kayak Fish Fighting

360 degree fight

You do not need to fight a monster fish from your kayak to have a lot of fun, and to enjoy the advantages of kayakfishing. Kayaking is already a great day on the water. Add the possibility of a fish, and the prospects for the day improve greatly. Add a few fish and the recipe is only sweeter. Hooking big fish and even monster fish from a kayak, though it is the stuff that goes into fantasies, is more than possible. It is probable, considering all of the advantages of fishing by kayak. So, you should be more than expectant of hooking into something big, and you should be prepared and knowledgeable in the ways of conducting a battle from your kayak. You should be confident, knowing that there are some definite advantages as well as enjoyments to fighting fish from a kayak.

Paddling a kayak along a shoreline with a light flyrod dropping bugs or flies into pockets where greedy little fish are waiting to gobble them up is a great way to spend a morning or an evening, putting a bend in your rod and a vibrating hum in your flyline. An ultralight spinning rod is nice too, and it turns tiny fish into tigers. Cruising along and poking tiny lures or bait into small pockets of aquatic vegetation with a canepole can be a lot of simple fun, especially when that long and limber pole comes to life, and out plucks a beautiful fishy gem in the form of a crappie or another species of the many panfish in freshwater. A kayak gives you a new perception of fighting a fish. Even an average fish. A kayak gets you closer to the action, closer to nature and closer to the fish. From your new perspective, you may even get a little water splashed in your face. Maybe more than a little.

But bigger fish are definitely more exciting, and of course, bigger is a relative word. A fish can be big for the tackle you are using, big for the situation you are in, the biggest one you've ever caught, very big, too big to bring into your kayak, or too big to mess with in your kayak. Big fish present some special challenges to a fisherman in a kayak. The challenges can vary according to whether you are fishing shallow or deep, whether or not there are any obstructions in the area, and according to the species you have hooked. The degree of difficulty will be influenced by such other factors as the size of your tackle in comparison to the size of the fish and the environment.

Once you hook a big fish, it is going to run, dive or jump. A few smart ones will run right back at you sometimes even before you can get the hook set well enough. In deep water, some fish are likely to dive as deep as they can get. Shallow water fish will probably run, and some species can run far and long. The jumpers often get away, especially the ones that run back at you first, but if they do not get free, they usually tire more quickly. Most big fish get away right at the beginning of a very short fight or at the end of a very long fight.

Watery sleigh ride

If you lose your fish early, the odds will be that the culprit will be an insufficient hookset. The next threat is a break off. Obviously, the probability of a break off rises sharply around obstructions and heavy weedcover. If you are in the shallows with a powerful and fast fish, you could get *spooled* and broke off. Of course, the hook could fall out at any time, especially if the fish continues to jump. The longer the fight continues, the bigger the hole wears where the hook is attached. If the fight goes too long, the fishing line will begin to wear and weaken. Even heavy shock tippets can give way to abrasive body parts after a time. As the fish begins to tire, it will become more desperate and begin to circle your kayak and even dive under it at midship often with startling bursts of revitalized energies, putting you at an awkward disadvantage. It will probably even get down and dirty, splashing water in your eyes before taking off on another run.

You can be a startled spectator during all of these shenanigans or be proactive on your own behalf, and a kayak has some great advantages to aid you during the battle. A kayak has its own backup drag system for your reel. Even a strong 4 or 5 lb. fish can tow your kayak around. If your drag is too tight or your reactions are too slow, the fish will still have a difficult time breaking the line in open water environments. If your rod is very stiff and your line is light for the fish, you could break it off. But with a well matched rod to line weight, the odds are against the fish. The principal is the same whether you are fishing heavier tackle for very large fish, medium size tackle for medium range fish, or even if you unexpectedly hook something very large on light tackle.

If you can get away with a slightly softer tip action, you can give yourself a little extra insurance. Just be certain that your rod is stiff enough to get the hook set on the species of fish you are targeting and strong enough to lift the fish out of deep water when it sounds. If your tackle is very light, then you want to increase line capacity to allow for longer runs. In open water, a 6 lb. test line spinning outfit should have about 250 yards of line or more. On a 10 lb. test outfit 200 yards will be fine. A baitcasting outfit, with a 7 to 7 1/2 ft. rod, with a medium to heavy action and 20 lb. test line, should have about 200 yards. The 20 lb. line will allow you to be towed in your kayak for hours without breaking. Unless you are planning to go offshore to fish for marlin, swordfish, or bluefin tuna those three outfits will handle just about anything you would be willing to bring up next to your kayak, and that includes some hefty inshore sharks and tarpon.

If you do nothing more than hang onto your rod, you may eventually wear a fish down by taking a *watery sleigh ride*. However, the longer the fight lasts, the higher the odds are raised for an escape. The flesh where the hook is lodged may tear. The hole may widen and the hook may fall out, especially if the fish jumps. Lighter lines will weaken after a time with much stress on them. Shock tippets and leaders get abrasive wear. Besides, you could get towed to another state, and some fish can actually revive while towing your kayak.

To shorten the fight, you will need to change the kayak from the towing position to the broadside position using pressure from the force of fighting the fish to turn the kayak. It is easy to accomplish this maneuver with a shorter and more maneuverable kayak. If you have a sit-on-top kayak, you can use the *paddle-on your-lap-technique* to aid you at times to fine tune your positioning. If your kayak has rudders, you can use them to great advantage against the fish. From the broadside position, the kayak will be much harder to tow. You can then exert far more pressure on the fish. If the fish goes on a long line stealing run, you can use the *rod pressure* to move back to the the towing position until you recapture enough line to return to the broadside position again.

Maneuvering broadside

Battling broadside

When a fish slows down and begins to sulk or dive without struggling to escape or run, don't allow it to rest. It may revive, causing the struggle to last even longer. You can usually get a fish to renew its struggle by giving it a few sharp jab strokes of the fishing rod tip, encouraging it to get moving. If the fish has stalled deeper down and refuses to respond to the jab strokes, move over top of its position and begin lifting to the surface. When a fish stalls close to the kayak and out to the side but near the surface, it is often effective to use a *low blow* to roll the fish over, usually followed by a line gaining lift toward the kayak. To execute a low blow, use a rod position low to the water and sweep the pole backward from the fish's head to the tail.

When the fish gets closer, it may begin to stubbornly circle

Sometimes they

Get behind you

Desperate fish

Awkward position

your kayak. This is a great oppurtunity to further tire the fish. By holding your rod low and pointing toward the bow, the fish will be forced to turn the kayak making it work even harder. A strong fish on a longer line may actually get behind you. That's okay. Simply raise your rod over your head, making sure that you keep pressure on the rod tip and on the fish. Also make sure that you clear any rods that may be standing upright in rodholders behind your seat. Allow the fish to circle around until it is broadside. If the fish is up near the surface, you may want to consider reversing the direction of force and giving the fish a *low blow* as previously discussed which often helps to defeat them psychologically. Or, you may return to making the fish fight the kayak by *turning* or *broadsiding*. Of course, if the fish responds like a champion as they often do with a line peeling run, you can revert to *towing* and start the process over.

Eventually the fish will be close at hand and desperate. Often in such situations, they will dive under your kayak at midship and leave you fighting them from that least favored position with your rod bent under the kayak and on the wrong side. At times like these, you will appreciate a short kayak and a long rod. Simply reach forward, clearing the bow, and resume fighting on the more enjoyable side of the kayak. If you are fishing out of a 14 footer, you will need both a long arm and a long rod. Have fun.

Many of the fish that like to jump during a fight will have one jump reserved for the end of the battle. Some save a couple. If you are using treble hooks, guard against that jump terminating in your lap. Toothy critters such as barracuda sometimes make a pass at your nose. If you are battling a tarpon or other high jumping fish with some body mass, you may want to bring along your football or German soldier helmut (see Chapter 15: *Kayakfishing Safety*).

Battles of this type in open water can cover a lot of water and often do not end up in the same area where they began. Everything may go well and according to plan until you encounter obstructions in the water that the fish can hang up on, tangling the line, and perhaps breaking off. The towing advantage that you have over fish while fighting them in open water can quickly turn against you around obstructions. When that big one you've lassoed starts heading for the channel marker to wrap around, it is in your best interest to start to do something about it early. And if you are casting to fish that are hiding in obstructive cover such as mangroves or fallen trees, a powerful fish can pull you in there to join it. To make matters worse, most of the obstructions in saltwater environments have sharp edged barnacles growing on them. Fortunately, there are a few things that you can do or, at least, try.

Shock tippets installed at the end of your fishing line will not

Trouble with trebles

only protect against break offs due to rough or sharp areas on fish, but also will give some protection against rough cover and obstructions such as branches, logs, dock pilings, rocks, concrete, oysters, and barnacles. Regular fishing line will not last long when pulled against these surfaces, especially under pressure. A shock tippet will also give you an extra measure of control over a fish at the end of a fight because *you can grab the line* without fear of it breaking. A shock tippet can be as short or long as you like or need. It can be simple or extravagant. It can be a simple 10-24 inches of anything from 20-100 lb. test, or it can be a series of increasingly heavier sections going toward the hook. It can be connected by a series of bloodknots that will pass easily through the guides. It can be over a rod length long, but usually, you do not want to wind it onto the reel. Such a shock tippet can give great protection when fishing around barnacle covered obstructions that would sever a connection between you and your fish instantaneously without it.

Even with the best shock tippets installed, obstructions create a formidable hazard, but there are some ways of dealing with them that will turn some of the odds to your favor. Sometimes when you try to force a fish such as a snook away from a barnacle covered obstruction such as a piling or a concrete bridge abutment, the fish will get an early jump on you and dive behind the obstruction before you can prevent it. In some instances, if the hook is already set, it is more effective to go to the obstruction. Leave the line slack. When you get around to the side the fish is on, resume the fight. Forcing the fight with the line wrapped around the barnacle covered obstruction would only guarantee a cutoff.

If you hook a strong fish out in the open but in the vincinity of an obstruction such as marker piling, buoy, crab pot, log or whatever, eventually the fish will probably head for it. If the fish heads away, go with it as far as the fish will go, but if the fish stalls or stays in the area, sooner or later it will swing by the obstruction. It may sound crazy but while the fish is still green, it sometimes pays off to go to the marker or obstruction before the fish does. The natural instinct of the fish is to get away from you. As the fish begins to tire, move away from the object. If the fish wants to make a long run, let it go and follow. Finish the fight in a safer area. Understand in advance however that Murphy's Law runs rampant in this type situation.

Trying to force a strong fish away from cover in a kayak that the fish is able to tow is a game rigged in favor of the fish. While casting to logs, docks, overhanging trees or mangroves for big largemouth bass or snook, it often comes down to a bluff. A game of psychology. Seconds and inches. If you can convince the fish that it is not going to get back into the cover, and it had better high tail for deeper water, then you have a chance. It's only a bluff, and it is a short lived game. The fish can tow you and your kayak into the cover if it sticks with the plan. There are a few other things that you can do, but you will have very little time, if any, to make up your mind and choose one.

You can toss your anchor out and hope for an immediate hold on the bottom. It happens. Sometimes. If you are really fast, you bluff and toss at the same time. It would require that you have the anchor at-the-ready to toss at any time. And of course, if you know a spot where you are likely to hook a good fish, you could set the anchor before casting to the fish. You might even try using a stake through one of your scupper holes. Texas kayakfishing guide Allen Cartmell uses this technique to hold a kayak stationary in shallow water (see Chapter 16: *Kayakfishing Experts*). Another more difficult maneuver is to immediately hop out of the kayak. Of course, the water must be shallow, the bottom must be solid, and you must be wearing a bowline attached to your belt to prevent your kayak from drifting away or you and your prize may have to walk home. Also, you must be using a sit-on-top kayak and be careful not to turn it over if there is any tackle or gear that are not fastened down.

Another option would be to hop out of the kayak when approaching a particularly promising area. Wading is a great way to get control of fish in heavy cover because your feet are firmly planted, and you can walk backward, forward or sideways to gain an advantage. It gets a little sloppy sometimes when required to run.

There are situations where being towed into cover is actually an advantage. When using heavy line in freshwater lakes, a big fish will become entangled in the heavy weedcover and discontinue the struggle, allowing the angler to approach and retrieve the fish along with a major mass of vegetation. Using heavy line, a kayaker need not even use the paddle. Rod pressure alone can pull you to the fish even through heavy vegetation. The newer braided lines such as Berkley FireLine or SpiderWire Braid are a formidable combination with a kayak for pulling big fish out of heavy cover. Some anglers would prefer to fight a big fish out in the open, but most anglers mainly want a trophy fish in the boat and close up battles on heavy tackle with big fish can be awsome with vegetative debris and water flying everywhere. On the other hand, some amazing feats can be accomplished with a medium action spinning rod and ten pound test, even in the weeds. Just do not try to force a weed-tangled fish toward your kayak. Go to the fish.

Chapter Fourteen

Kayak Fish Handling

Get the gaff

Okay, you've battled the big fish down, and it is up next to the kayak, what next? Well, that depends. It depends upon your intentions. Are you going to release the fish? Keep it? Eat it? Mount it? It also depends upon what type of fish it is. How big is it? More importantly, how big are the teeth? It depends upon what type of hooks you are using. Any fish can be dangerous with a set or more of treble hooks hanging from its mouth. It especially depends upon what type of epquipment you have to handle the fish. Do you have a net, a gaff, jaw gripping pliers, or gloves? Is there another boat nearby to help you? It depends upon the environmental set up. Is the water deep? Are there shallows nearby? Land? And it depends upon your kayak's storage characteristics. Is there a place for a cooler? Is there a large storage area for a big fish? Is there a large hatch opening?

Now what

Releasing your fish is the most convenient way to handle your fish. It is also the most *conservation-friendly*. In addition, you will not need ice or a cooler. If you have a cooler onboard your kayak, releasing your fish will allow you to use your cooler for other storage purposes. For the purposes of conservation, you should have a pair of surgical forceps onboard to unhook more delicate species such as trout or panfish with tiny mouths such as bluegill. A pair of needlenose pliers works great for most other species, except for some of the critters that are a little long in the tooth. For more dangerous mouthed individuals, you may want to carry a longer set of needlenose pliers. You may also want to keep your fingers a little further from sharp sets of treble hooks wielded wildly about by an otherwise harmless catch. Some guys carry a notched broom handle for removing a hook from the mouth of a shark.

In some cases, it is safer for you and the fish to simply cut the line. With a sharp knife you can quickly cut the line close to the hook. The hook will fall out after several days, if not sooner, in saltwater environments. It is best not to remove large fish from the water when your intention is to release them. The stress of prolonged handling, and the effects of gravity on internal organs is not safe for a large fish that you intend to release. If the fish happens to be a shark, it is also safer for you to release the fish by cutting the line with a *long* sharp knife. The longer the knife, the safer your hand.

Non dangerous fish that you intend to release and that are safe to handle should be given every chance to survive. Take the extra time required to fully resuscitate them before releasing them. Sometimes they will swim out of your hand but then sink to the bottom and die. They need to keep moving to move water over their gills in order to transfer enough oxygen to their bloodstream. Redfish, in particular, tend to hide in the grass when released too early and need to be prodded into motion repeatedly.

Lightweight hooks that will straighten under heavy stress are an effective method of releasing long and hard fighting fish. The technique is especially effective on large tarpon when fished on light tackle. They give a great fight with lots of spectacular jumps, and then when the fish dives and persists in a long drawn out and gruesome tug of war, you can put a real strain on the rod during a run as the fish is heading straight away. The hook straightens out, and the fish gets away. It is a convenient technique when there are more tarpon around, and you want to hook another fresh one. You do not have to build a new shock tippet or tie on a new hook. You simply rebend the hook back into shape with your needlenose pliers. Pinching down the barb will also help to exit the battle early. This method of release is the least stressful on the fish.

Surprisingly, a gaff can be used to aid in the release of a large fish. A fish can be gaffed with minimal damage and be released. Of course, you would not want to gaff the fish in the body. You would either gaff the fish under the chin or slip the gaff under the gill cover in the chin area and out the mouth. You can then pin the fish to the side of the kayak which will effectively immobilize it and will reduce stress due to struggling. It will also aid your efforts for a quick release.

If you wish to actually land or boat your fish, then shock tippets installed at the end of your fishing line and attached to your lure or hook will aid you a great deal. In addition to preventing break offs due to sharp teeth or abrasive body parts, the shock tippet will allow you to get your fish under control quickly at the side of your kayak. You will be able to safely grab the leader without fear of break offs. By holding the leader, it will be easier to net, lip or gaff the fish. Depending upon the strength of your shock tippet and the size of your fish, you can usually pull your fish directly onboard by holding the shock tippet. Shock tippets are normally used only in saltwater where the fish are not usually leader shy.

Probably the most popular, convenient and effective way to land non sharp toothed fish is to grip the fish by the lower jaw. The technique is commonly called *lipping*. The lipping technique is especially effective because it has an immobilizing effect on the fish, and it requires no additional epquipment other than your hand. It is the most commonly used technique on largemouth bass, crappie and snook. Of course, if the fish has sharp teeth, the technique cannot be used without a gripping device such as The Lipper (see photo on page 109). With a gripping device and a long pair of needlenose pliers, you can unhook a large toothy critter such as a muskellunge, northern pike or barracuda with a minimum of risk from teeth or treble hooks. A gripping device is also safer to use to grip the lower jaw on non toothy fish that have a plug full of treble hooks in their mouth which can be just as dangerous as the teeth.

Some fish have a few sharp teeth, but can be seized behind the gills. Seatrout, bluefish and jack crevalle in saltwater can be handled easily in this manner. In freshwater, it's a great way to grab toothy chain pickerel and small pike. Larger specimens may be too large for your hand to get a grip in this area, or they may have sharp edged gills or dorsal spines that interfere with gaining your grasp on the fish without damaging your hand.

Resuscitating a tarpon

Gloves are convenient to carry along and very helpful for dealing with many fish that have small teeth, sharp or rough areas in the mouth or on other body parts. Striped bass and snook both have razor-like sharp edges on areas of their gill covers. Jack crevalle have a sharp edged area near the anal opening. If you should ever join the elite group that has hooked into a billfish by kayak, you may discover how rough the bill can be. On a live thrashing fish, you will want to be wearing gloves. Many fish have sharp projections or a crushing ability in the gill areas. Redfish, black drum, striped bass, and bonefish have dangerous gill areas that should be avoided even with gloves.

Nets are not convenient to carry along, but convenient to use when a fish is alongside your kayak. A net gets the fish under control quickly and helps to resuscitate a fish during and after the hook removal process. In some states, the use of a landing net is required by law and when properly done is a conservation friendly technique. One great alternative to carrying a conventional landing net is to make a floating flyfishing stripping basket/landing net/fish holder/resuscitator (see also Chapter 10: *Kayak Flyfishing*). Since it is made with a soft foam, it can be placed behind your seat as a cushion if your seat backs up against your cooler. If you store it below the deck inside the kayak, it will aid your kayak as a flotation device. It attaches to your kayak via velcro straps and can be set over the side or set into the kayak while attached. One of the nicest features of this floating basket is that a fish can be left sitting in the basket with or without the hook attached after the fight to allow the fish to recover before release. In the meantime, while the fish catches its breath, you can get your camera out. Unfortunately, it is only practical for fish up to roughly 10-12 lbs.

Gaffing is the best way to go with large fish when you know that you intend to kill the fish, especially dangerous fish. A longer two handed gaff is preferrable to hold the fish away from you. It is best to gaff the fish near the head to prevent it from turning to bite you. However, you want to wait until the fish is oriented away from you because the sting of the gaff usually results in the fish thrusting in a forward motion. You do not want to be positioned in front of the fish at that time. You want to wait to hit them with the gaff when they are going away from you. Sharks in particular due to their cartilagenous spinal cord are able to turn their bodies in an extreme fashion that can surprise an angler, catching him off guard and delivering a vicious bite. Make sure the fish is dead before bringing it into your kayak. Sharks often appear to be dead and then suddenly revive. Some fish such as cobia are known for fighting harder in the boat than in the water. They are large, strong, and capable of doing much damage. It is also best to fight a large fish until it is exhausted before attempting to gaff it from a kayak. Large fish are very powerful and will react violently to the strike of a gaff. It is best to learn the most effective kill zone for striking with the gaff, and you need a gaff with a large enough hook to penetrate deeply into the fish, damaging internal organs. Sharks are usually dispatched more quickly when gaffed deeply into the gill area. Cobia are some-times killed quickly when gaffed from underneath and out through the top of the head. In order for your gaff to penetrate well, you should triangulate the gaff point with a file similar to how it is done with a hook point. If you plan to catch and keep a large fish in your kayak, you should carry a hammer in your kayak to fin-ish killing the fish before handling it. A number of sharp blows to the head usually get the job done. If you plan to mess around with sharks much from your kayak, you should carry a bangstick which will dicharge a shotgun load into the head when the shark gets alongside your kayak.

A flying gaff works well if you want to tow the fish to a more favorable area to land it. A flying gaff detaches from the handle but stays connected to the angler by a rope. A barb on the gaff hook prevents the fish from escaping. Big boat anglers will often tie off the rope to a cleat. Kayakfishermen can install a RHYNOBAR (see photo on page 102). In a kayak, however, a fisherman should first consider if possibly the fish is too big for the kayak. You can install a float and a quick release clip on the rope so that you can release the rope if the fish makes a strong run that may frighten or threaten you. At first, when the fish is gaffed, you can hold onto the rope. Then, as the fish tires and dies, you can attach the rope to the kayak using a quick release mechanism. The fish can then be towed, preferably backwards, to the nearest beach. Some anglers like to slip a noose over the tail. The tail noose will severely hinder the fish from swimming and struggling. Usually the fish will die when treated in this man-ner. The quick release is important for your safety if the fish becomes too wild or if it comes under attack by sharks. In some areas of fresh and saltwater in the United States, it is very pos-sible for a battling fish to come under attack by an alligator, and in some other countries and continents crocodiles must be con-sidered, depending on the location.

Whether you use a flying gaff or a conventional gaff, it is re-ally helpful if you can plan to hook your fish near land where you can battle the fish closer to shore to land it. It could also be an island or even a sandbar temporarily exposed at low tide. Even shallows and shoals are helpful if they are shallow enough to beach or immobilize the fish. Even if you can reduce the swimming to wallowing, it will give you an advantage. You may want to hop out of the kayak to finish off the fish, but if it is a shark or barracuda, then you will want to gaff and kill the fish first.

Some California kayakfishermen have a safe alternative for dealing with large sharks. When they hook a large shark and battle it down to the finish, they flag a nearby larger boat and request assistance. Apparently, the curiousity of other fishermen toward big fish and kayaks doing battle is enough to warrant time out to lend a hand, and they cannot resist becoming a part of the the obvious big fish tale being played out before their eyes. The finishing touches are put to the shark from the relative safety of the larger boat. These guys are doing battle with some major size thresher sharks. If you have a larger boat, you can use it to transport your kayak to the fishing grounds and then launch your kayak to do the actual fishing. After hooking and wearing down an upsized behemoth of one species or another, you can scramble back aboard the bigger boat for the gaffing ceremony.

I will describe but not recommend here a technique that some kayakfishermen are using to pull sharks onboard, remove the hook with a notched broomstick, and release them. Some sharks can be grabbed by the tail and pulled partially onboard the kayak without them turning sharply to bite you. George Whillock in Alabama uses the technique successfully on blacktips, but he says that some other sharks will turn and bite you. Jim Sammons of La Jolla Kayak Fishing cautions that this is a *cutting edge* technique and should be used by experienced kayakfishermen only. The technique usually involves getting a rope around the shark's tail to neutralize the sharks mobility and using a notched broomstick to remove the hook.

Once you have whipped a fish that you intend to keep, you will need a place to store it. Smaller fish are not much of a problem. If you have a cooler installed or a livewell, you are in great shape. If you want to keep the fish fresh in the cooler, you will need to have ice. If you do not have ice, your fishing time will be very limited if you want to get the fish home fresh. There are a few things that you can do, however, to stretch your time window. The fish should be kept as cool as possible. Of course, the weather will be the biggest factor, but the fish should be kept out of the sun, wet, and where a breeze can promote evaporation which has a cooling effect. In a sit-on-bottom kayak, a fish can be set inside the kayak with a wet towel over it. If the spray skirt is off, it will get some circulation of air. In sit-on-top kayaks, you can lay a fish in the flooded footwells with a towel or t-shirt wrapped around it. The t-shirt not only keeps the fish wet all over

Stunning grip

and shaded from the sun, but it also helps to keep the fish from flopping all over, especially overboard.

Bigger fish create bigger problems. Large fish can be wrapped in towels or netting and can be strapped to the deck of a sit-on-bottom kayak. On sit-on-top kayaks, you can lay the dead fish on a concave forward deck, and it will ride rather nicely without strapping in place. On sit-on-top kayaks with a large enough hatch opening, you can slip a large fish right inside the kayak for safe keeping and to get it out of the sun. It is best to keep the hatch cover off to allow air to circulate below deck until you can get the fish back to shore and onto ice quickly. It is a good idea to carry a burlap bag to keep the fish wet and to control fish slime below deck. Depending on how long it will take you to get back to shore, you may want to bleed your shark to keep it fresh, and it might be advisable to bleed it into the kayak interior to avoid exciting too many sharks with a blood trail leading to your kayak. Of course, after such a great catch, you shouldn't mind too much the extra chore of washing out the interior of the kayak with a hose. Someone will eventually design and sell a larger, longer insulated dry bag capable of storing a 3 to 4 foot (or longer) fish below decks with ice. There is presently a company, Muleworks Inc., selling a 22x12x9 inch insulated dry bag named The Icemule Cooler (see Chapter 17: *Kayakfishing Resources*).

If you tow your fish back to port with a rope or with your flying gaff rope, you will be presenting a temptation to sharks, especially if the fish is bleeding. If you choose that option, make sure you use a quick release attachment so you can separate yourself from your prize if the sharks decide they want it more than you do. For the same reason, it is not advisable to throw a stringer of smaller fish overboard to keep them. In southern states, a stringer of fish is a temptation to an alligator in freshwater environs. Under most circumstances, alligators would never bother you in a kayak. However, they occasionally do challenge fishermen in their canoes for a fish they hook. You do not want to become a footnote in an animal behavior book. Let them have it.

George Whillock with a big blacktip onboard

Chapter Fifteen

Kayak Fishing Safety

This book is not intended to be the last word or an authority on kayakfishing safety. This chapter is intended to share with you some information gained by experience and research. This chapter is not written with the intent to scare you but to prepare you for some things that you may not be aware of or have experience with. Kayakfishing is a fairly new and developing sport. The safety parameters for various fishing environments, techniques, and target species are yet being developed. To learn more about sit-on-top kayaking and kayaking safety you should also read a copy of Tom Holtey's book *Sit-On-Top Kayaking*. Nature, outdoor environments, weather, water, and wild creatures are all unpredictable. No amount of information can prepare you for all possibilities. Be careful out there.

Weather

Weather should always be checked and taken into account for all your trip planning. It is important in considering your fishing prospects and plans as well as for your own safety. Safety considerations with weather are most often centered around storm activity. The two most common and violent causes for storm activity are frontal conditions and summer thunderstorm activity. Low pressure areas can also create storms which can develop into very serious tropical storms or even hurricanes. A casual glance at the weather report occasionally will alert you to tropical storms and hurricanes. Only the most unprepared individuals will be caught out in such weather events.

Unless you watch the weather regularly, you could get caught out in a frontal situation where cold air moving down from the north meets warmer southern air masses. The greater the difference in the air temperatures where they meet usually determines the severity of the storms. The important thing to remember is when it is scheduled to hit in your area, and to remember that it is only a prediction. Some types of fishing such as largemouth bass fishing are at their best right before a front passes and deteriorate once the cold front moves in. It would be wise to be well informed of the weather prediction and be prepared for an early arrival of the front. It would also be wise to choose a fishing location that would not leave you at high risk to rough weather conditions.

Summer thunderstorms are more difficult to avoid because they are often in the forecast for each day of the summer. The probability, size, and severity for a specific location are actually pretty unpredictable; more like a coin toss, and they can suddenly and unpredictably get severe and widespread. Isolated thunderstorms over water can suddenly grow larger and more intense. They often join with other less severe storm cells, forming a chain and intensifying. They can be very unpredictable in their direction, shifting to one direction and then another for hours before moving on.

Wind

The two main threats to a kayaker in storms are wind and lightening. Wind, of course, means rough water which creates a potential for drowning. However, kayaks can take quite a bit of rough water, especially when paddled by an experienced kayaker. The key is not to allow the waves to catch you broadside. If a big wave hits you broadside, it can turn you over. You want to keep the bow or the stern directed at an angle toward the waves. You want to be wearing a life preserver. You should wear a bowline with a quick release clip attached to your belt. If you are tumbled over, you will not be separated from your kayak. If your kayak has a half dozen swimming noodles inside(see Chapter 7: *Kayakfishing Accessories*), it will not sink. If your kayak is a stable model, it will be easy to reboard. The most important thing is not to panic. Stay with your kayak even if you are unable to reboard.

Actually, kayakers have a special advantage to avoid rough water and life threatening situations. Kayaks can paddle waters so shallow that they are unable to create a wave more than a few inches. The route by shallows may not be the shortest route, but it is pretty hard to get yourself drowned in such situations. When the weather has any chance of getting ugly, do not commit yourself to paddle large expanses of open deep water.

Lightening

Lightening is probably more frightening to most people. If not when the storm is approaching, then definitely once it starts cracking around you. You can expect lightening from both frontal situations moving into your area and also from the typical summer afternoon thunderstorms. Get a head start when you see potential trouble approaching. While you are on the water, if you hear a faint vibrating or buzzing sound coming from your fishing rods and if your fishing line seems to be floating upward into the air like a long silky spider web in the wind, get off the water. The ions in the air are highly charged, and a lightening strike could hit any time. While you are still paddling for shore, lower your rods from upright rodholders because they will act as lightening rods. Stay away from anything metal that could conduct electricity. Use an all plastic or wood paddle if you have one for a spare. When you reach shore, do not stand upright, especially out in the open. You do not want to be the tallest object in your area which would make you the lightening rod. Do not stand next to or under trees which are natural lightening rods. If you are caught out in the open, stoop down but do not lie down. You want to stay low but reduce your contact with the ground.

Fog

Another common weather related threat is fog. Fog can get you lost and can leave you open to the threat of being struck by a larger boat, which becomes even more probable when you are lost. It is best to stay off larger waters where there are motorized craft when fog is present. It is also a good idea to stay in close contact with a shoreline to prevent getting disoriented and traveling in circles. You should be observant toward landmarks such as water towers or other permanent features. And of course, if you are paddling on larger bodies of water, you should have a compass or a GPS unit onboard.

Overexposure to the elements

Overexposure to the elements is another weather related concern. When the water or air temperatures are cold, the body loses heat unless you wear insulated clothing to conserve your body's heat. Otherwise, your body's metabolism will become overtaxed trying to warm a body that can't hold the heat. A condition known as *hypothermia* can sneak up on you without you realizing it. The weather or water does not have to be freezing. It just has to be significantly lower than your body temperature for an extended period of time. Since the body temperature is 98.6 degrees, hypothermia can occur after an extended period in 70 degree water. Hypothermia is one of the most common conditions treated by rescue professionals, and the incidents are escalating as people increasingly take part in outdoor sports. It can be life threatening if not treated promptly.

When using a sit-on-top kayak for kayakfishing in cool weather or waters, you should wear neoprene waders with a water repellant jacket or a wetsuit to keep your body insulated. The wetsuit will keep you warm and insulated, but the neoprene waders and jacket will also keep you dry. Wear a hat because most of your body heat is lost through your head. Make sure the neoprene waders fit your body snugly, wear suspenders, and a belt tightly around your waist over the waders. The belt will help to keep water out of your waders if you take a spill. Also, do not wear bootfooted waders. Bootfooted waders will fill with water, and they will probably get you drowned. Wear the stocking footed neoprene waders with *dive booties*. They will be much easier to swim in if your kayak takes a spill. When fishing from a sit-on-bottom kayak, dress warm and dry. Have a rain jacket handy, and use a spray skirt to keep the interior of the kayak dry if the weather gets wet or the wind and waters get rough. Sit-on-bottom kayaks are usually preferred by kayakers in cooler northern waters and by kayakers who just like to stay dry.

When the body becomes seriously overheated, it is said to be suffering from *hyperthermia* which is also known as *heat prostration* or *heat stroke*. This condition can ultimately lead to death if not treated promptly. When the weather is hot out on the water, kayakfishermen should have plenty of extra water to drink onboard. They should also wear a hat and light, loose fitting clothing. You should also be careful about overly exerting yourself on extremely hot days. It helps to get at least a little wet which is not a hard thing to do in a kayak, especially a sit-on-top kayak.

Overexposure to the suns rays can result in an immediate, serious, and painful case of sunburn which can also result in *sun poisoning* where the skin may blister and ooze body fluid, resulting eventually in open sores. Long term neglect to adequately prevent exposure to the suns rays can result in skin cancer. Some forms of skin cancer can be fatal. Skin protection is a good habit. You should be in the habit of having the right protective clothing on board at all times. It should be easily accessible. Your sunblock should also be onboard at all times and also be easily accessible. Break the bad habit of making one more cast before covering up with long sleeves or applying sunblock because we all know that one more cast leads to one more and one more. More damage is done to skin in early mornings and windy, cool, cloudy days because it does not feel like there is damage being done, and fishermen do not take precautions until it is too late. One neat trick, when wearing shorts in summer, is to carry a lightweight bath towel. Use it to cover your legs when the sun's rays get too intense, and you can also wipe your hands on it.

Fish fighting

Getting closer to nature does not come without some increased risk. With such a low profile on the water, a kayak gets a fisherman closer to the prey than any other craft. As with all prey fighting for their lives, some extreme behavior is displayed. Fish with mouths full of sharp teeth or barbed treble hooks will launch into aerial displays with wild head shaking attempts to throw the hooks right back at you. Fish capable of leaping over your head may instead leap right into your lap. Should a bit of you get between their teeth, some of them will intentionally chomp down. While wading, you will often feel hooked fish run between your legs or crash into your shins if you close the gap to prevent them from taking advantage of you in such a manner. If that fish has a mouth full of treble hooks in crotch deep water, well, you can use your imagination. It is a good idea to restrict the use of treble hooks and to look for good single hook alternatives to, at least, reduce the risk involved with their use.

Handling the fish at the end of a fight also has some inherent danger involved with those same teeth and treble hooks as well as some other sharp or spiny areas on many species of fish. In addition, there are some logistical problems with the decisions about where to put the fish. In a larger boat, you often simply sweep them aboard and dump them on the floor till they calm down. In a kayak, that is usually your last option or no option, depending on the size of the teeth and the size of the fish. Sometimes an unusually large misbehaving specimen will hurl itself into your kayak which is already occupied by you. You need to have the right gear available to quickly deal with fish, especially potentially harmful fish at the side of your kayak. (see Chapter 13: *Kayak Fishfighting* and Chapter 14: *Kayak Fish Handling*).

Scary critters

Aside from the fish that you pick a fight with, there are some other creature threats more or less real and imagined. Alligators are rarely a serious threat, especially to canoers and kayakers.

Most alligator attacks do not involve alligators out in the wild; but instead, gators that have had a lot of contact with people. In fact, they are usually gators that have been fed by people. As a result, they equate people with food. One day when there is no food, they eat the people. Unfortunately, the people they eat are usually the little people. Kids, especially toddlers allowed to be alone by the bankside, are often taken. Dogs are another of their favorites. Adults are attacked under unusual circumstances such as snorkeling or scuba diving through weedy areas of their territory where it is thought they are mistaken for rival gators in a territorial tresspassing situation. Not smart, especially in breeding season when the males are particularly aggressive toward one another. Another rare but possible circumstance occurs when a small boater such as a canoer hooks a fish. The gator sees the struggling, easy meal and goes for it. Of course, it ends up closer to you. Let the gator have the fish.

While wading, as long as you keep your boat or kayak attached to you by a rope so that it travels along with you, the gators will keep their distance. Once in a while, you will see a curious one watch or follow you. Sometimes in breeding season, a gator will puff itself up, float high on the water, and raise its tail. It's a threat. Mostly, a bluff. Usually from a good distance. In your kayak, you are bigger looking and tougher looking. The gator will be very content to let you pass by unmolested. Gators get much bolder at night, however. Don't drag around stringers of dead fish, and don't wade at night.

Sharks are probably more of a threat in your imagination than they are in reality. Unless, of course, you hook one and pull it up to your kayak. And that is your decision. There are a few places that I know, however, that I will not go to in my kayak even if I'm fishing for sharks. If you do not want incidents with sharks, be careful of creating any blood trails in the water, do not drag any fish around on a stringer, and if you are fighting a fish on your line when a shark suddenly attacks it, let him have all of it. Sit quiet til he's done and gone.

What's really scary

Probably more of a threat comes in a much smaller package. Almost everyone is afraid of snakes. Usually it is unwarranted, but in the case of water moccassins, perhaps it is warranted. At least, in a kayak and in their quiet domain before your blundering intrusion. They sometimes seem truly offended when you invade their quiet sanctuary, and they swim out to meet you, seemingly without the slightest bit of fear. In a boat with higher side rails, they would still be worriesome. In a kayak, such a meeting would be frightening. They often have the habit of hanging in tree limbs over the water. When boats pass by, they panic and dive into the water. Sometimes they land right in the boat which results in all hands doing what appears to be an ancient snake dance all over the boat. There is no room to snake dance in a kayak. Watch out for overhanging trees in moccassin country. And if you accidentally come across a swimming moccassin in a quiet little backwater, paddle quickly in reverse, and assume it will aggressively defend its territory.

Most dangerous creatures

Actually, the most frightening and most dangerous creatures on the water are your common everyday people when they climb into big mean powerboats, and there are a lot of them out there. You need to take some precautions. The primary defense is to avoid the areas where they are commonly found such as boating channels and high traffic areas. The main threat is being run over by one, and they seem to have particularly bad vision, often engaging in mutually destructive maneuvers. Seriously though, you really should paddle a brightly colored kayak to lessen the chance of not being noticed until it is too late to avoid hitting you. If the area you are paddling has rolling waves that intermittently hide your presence in the valleys between the crests of the waves, you should display a flag high above your kayak.

In most places that you kayak, you will be safe from powerboats if you stay in very shallow or very weedy water, except in areas where airboats are commonly used. Airboats can navigate your lawn if you spray the garden hose on it. When your kayak is behind emergent vegetation such as sawgrass, reeds or cattails, they cannot see you. Unfortunately, for kayakers, airboats often run right over such vegetation without a second thought. Make sure you are not behind that vegetation when they come roaring by.

Night paddling involves an even greater threat from airboats in the shallows and conventional boats elsewhere. You should carry a bright light to get their attention when any boat is in your area. One guy in New Jersey places a flashlight inside his bright yellow kayak which lights up the kayak like a lantern at night time.

Safety epquipment list:

life preserver
safety belt(attaches to bow line)
whistle
flare
compass
GPS
VHF radio/cell phone
flashlite
water
paddle leash
anchor
first aid kit
sunblock
raised visibility flags

Jeff "Rhyno" Krieger with a 52 lb. California white sea bass

Chapter Sixteen

Kayakfishing Experts

This group of experts is not meant to be a complete, but rather, a *growing* list. Besides, there is surely a long line of *Eskimo pros* going way back that had some stories to tell just before they got pulled under the ice, kayak and all. And there are probably plenty who lived to tell their fishing and hunting tales and died safe and warm in their own igloos. Well, maybe not. But we do have some modern day living legends such as Bill *Kayak Willie* Titler of Pompano Beach, Florida who is famous for entering prestigous sailfish tournaments and competing quite successfully from his kayak. There are many more experienced kayakfishermen out there quietly going about their sport. In fact, this author has met some of them on the water and learned a few things in the chance meetings. Regretfully, this author neglected to make the chance meetings a repeatable probability. From now on, he is taking names and numbers just as he has with the individuals listed below which he is more than happy to share with you. This group is a good cross section of the expert kayak anglers in the U.S. and Canada who are out there right now working out the techniques and details that are improving, refining, and defining our sport. The contact information for these individuals including addresses, phone numbers, email addresses and available websites can be found in Chapter 17: *Kayakfishing Resources.*

Mark Ambrozic

Mark Ambrozic is from Ontario, Canada. He has been kayakfishing since 1994. He seems to have followed the natural evolution of a kayakfisherman. Mark is not a kayaker turned fishermen. He grew up fishing from the family summer cottage dock. He started on foot, graduated to canoes, then to motorized craft, pulled back to tubefloats, and then, he found and eventually fell in love with kayaks for fishing. However, his kayakfishing career got off to a shakey start. He bought a used sit-on-bottom kayak from a local rental. Mark was immediately amazed with the kayak's maneuverability and stealth, and its ability to penetrate those normally inaccessible areas. He could travel greater distances with the kayak than he could with canoes. He found that he could drag a kayak back into the Canadian bush loaded with all of his gear like a sled and then get across the lake easily: unlike his experience with a tubefloat. However, his first attempt at actually fishing revealed some drawbacks. He didn't have a good, convenient place to put the rod while paddling, and he didn't have a convenient place for the paddle while fishing to keep it from falling overboard. One favorite method of fishing, trolling, was frustrating without a solution of where to safely and effectively station the rod while working with the paddle. Mark's first attempt to fish from his new kayak ended in comedic frustration and embarrassment. He shelved the kayakfishing idea. Fortunately, during a bout of cabin fever over the frozen Canadian winter, he came up with the solution to his kayakfishing endeavors. The First Mate was born that winter, and also his new company I.I. Endeavors.

The First Mate is a complete rod, paddle, tackle storage and trolling system for sit-on-bottom kayaks. It will allow you to carry up to four rods, a paddle, and tackle boxes conveniently, safely and securely on the deck in front of you. It will also allow you to position a rod for trolling without fear of it going overboard when the fish strikes. It attaches very easily to the kayak without any permanent alterations. With the First Mate, Mark was able to successfully pursue largemouth bass, smallmouth bass, muskie, pike, walleye, brown and rainbow trout by trolling, flyfishing, and with conventional casting tackle without fear of someone witnessing his former kayak comedy act. Instead, Mark regularly nails his favorite targets, Canadian largemouth and smallmouth bass to 22 inches and 20 inches respectively. He has also landed pike to 40 inches and rainbows to 16 inches. Mark fishes large lakes and small ponds as well as light flowing rivers and streams. Headquartered in Toronto, Mark's favorite lakes are the Muskoka and Kawartha lakes. Also, he fishes the Simcoe area lakes and stretches of the Ottawa River.

Mark Ambrozic with a big Canadian largemouth

Mark's main goal in kayakfishing is to develop kayaks into the ultimate fishing vessels and to introduce the benefits of kayakfishing to other fishermen. Mark's best advice to beginners is to rent a variety of kayaks to try out before settling on a model to purchase. He also advises fishermen to learn to kayak before trying to fish from a kayak. He likes the plastic kayaks for their light weight, durability and economical price. His favorite kayak is a sit-on-bottom model, the Paluski *Spirit*, because it is inexpensive, comfortable, and handles well. Mark has a website on the Internet where he promotes the First Mate and kayakfishing.

Gary Bulla

Gary Bulla is a kayak flyfisherman. He is not a newcomer to the sport. He has been kayak flyfishing since 1985 on the waters of the southern California coast and Baja waters. Gary has landed over 65 species of fish on a fly in saltwater, and he has caught as many as 10 different species on a fly in one day. An accomplished flytier, one of his designs was featured in *California Flyfisher* magazine. He guides and teaches saltwater flyfishing at home on the southern California coast, and he is one of the most active flyfishing guides on Baja waters. Several times a year he leads extended kayak flyfishing trips to Espiritu Santo Island where his groups catch a great variety of inshore gamefish.

In southern California waters, Gary's flyfishing catch usually includes barred surf perch, corbina, sea bass, halibut and at times striped bass. The striped bass are caught flyfishing the heavy surf from the beach and seem to occur only a couple times a month at secret locations near his home. Gary intends to try moving out past the the heavy surf to try for them by kayak. Gary also specializes in flyfishing the beach on foot as well as flyfishing bluewater from larger boats, but for fishing the waters of Baja and for fishing the kelp beds off the California coast, Gary uses a kayak.

In Baja waters, the kayak flyfishing catch may include green jacks, pargo, jack crevalle, topsail pompano, black skipjack, Pacific bonita, and a wide variety of other species in the Sea of Cortez. On the Pacific central coast of Baja, Gary fishes the mangrove estuaries of Magdelena Bay for grouper, corvina, halibut, and cabrilla. Gary has located a few snook there and is presently closing in on reported higher concentrations of them. He may include a kayak flyfishing trip to that location in the near future.

Gary started using a kayak to extend his fishing beyond the surf by exploring the inshore waters and the kelp beds off the California coast. Gary's favorite flyfishing kayak is a Cobra *Fisherman* which is a sit-on-top model. The deck is stripped down for easy flyfishing. He fishes in lagoons to 8 feet deep and over boulder reefs or bluewater to 30 feet deep. Long casts are really only important to let the sink tip get down, travel level and cover a nominal amount of area. Otherwise, in the mangrove lined lagoons long casts can help with shy snook. Gary uses 9 to 10 weight shooting taper lines with sinktips or interchangeable sink tips of 200 or 300 grains.

For flies, Gary's picks are chartreuse, silver and white Clousers, black and white Deceivers, Terry Baird's Deep Swimmer, Tres Generations, and his own design that was featured in Calfornia Flyfisher magazine, the Gremmie. His favorite color Gremmie is red. A Gremmie is a useful all purpose fly that can imitate baitfish, shrimp, crabs, or bloodworms. You can get the directions to tie up your own Gremmie or purchase Gremmies and other flies at Gary's website. He is also a master woodcraftsman, and he builds some beautiful and convenient flytying benches that are featured in Patagonia's flyfishing catalogue and are also illustrated and sold at his website.

Gary Bulla with a fly caught skipjack

Gary's favorite fish is the black skipjack because of the violent strikes, the long sizzling runs, the valiant fights to the last moment, and because they are available to kayak flyfishermen up to 10 lbs. One of Gary's main kayak flyfishing goals, however, is to spend more time exploring the mangroves of Magdelena

Bay on the Baja Pacific coast and some of the other islands in the Sea of Cortez, seeking out larger snook.

If you visit his website, you can also get a better glimpse at the unique and exotic kayak/flyfishing/camping adventures that Gary offers his clients. He takes his flyfishing seriously, but he is not just out there for the fish. Gary grew up on the beach and other waters of southern California. His curiosity, interest and enjoyment of the ocean and nature have contributed to his success as a flyfisherman. He is one of those guys who are going to catch a lot of fish because he likes being out there, and he enjoys observing and understanding the subtleties and details of what he observes. Fortunately, he practices and promotes catch and release. There is a chapter in Scott Sadil's book *Cast from the Edge*, titled "Good as Gold". It is about a week long visit he had with Gary in southern California. He is a flyfisherman first, but he is much more. He is also a master flytier, a wood craftsman, a naturalist, an explorer, and an instructor. But most importantly, he is a kayakfisherman.

Jim Sammons

Jim Sammons is a kayakfishing guide. He got into kayakfishing back in 1990 because he was tired of fishing from a surfboard off the San Diego, California coast. Jim wanted something more comfortable, faster, with greater range and with more storage than a surfboard. He couldn't afford a twenty foot center console, but a kayak seemed like a perfect fit. So, fishing from kayaks for marlin close to 200 lbs. and giant sharks over 172 lbs. is not such a stretch for Jim: it is for the rest of us. Most of us feel pretty extreme just catching our kelp bass, striped bass, and redfish from our kayaks.

Jim's favorite kayak is Ocean Kayak's *Scupper Pro* with the tank well. He likes it because it is fast, and because it has plenty of storage area. The tank well area is a great place for a cooler or a live bait tank. He says they are tough and will last for many years. He has installed a GPS unit and uses the portable Hummingbird fishfinder units to locate baitfish and bottom structure.

Jim uses the rocket launcher style rodholders with an aluminum base for strength. Jim rates his live bait tank as his number one accessory.

His tank will carry up to two dozen live mackerel and keep them alive all day. Jim says live bait fishing is the thing that has really brought big game fishing and kayakfishing together. He likes to use live mackerel and sardines, but sardines are a distant second. Live bait has increased his ability to catch the larger gamefish such as marlin, thresher sharks, and yellow tail.

Besides monster marlin and savage sharks, Jim also catches yellow tail, calico bass, barracuda, and bonito. Yellow tail are popular for their fighting ability and as table fare. A fifteen pounder is a nice one, but they can go over thirty. Calico bass are a favorite sport fish and can be caught year round. Jim has a lot of fun fighting barracuda which at times can be caught on every cast. Pound for pound, bonito fight as well as anything out there, and they take artificial lures well.

Jim's favorite lure choice depends upon what he's fishing for that day. For all around use, he likes plastic swimming baits such as a Fishtrap because they are so versatile. They can be trolled, cast, bounced or dragged off the bottom, and just about anything will eat them. For barracuda, he likes to use a heavy casting spoon with a single hook to simplify the release. For everyday trolling, Rapala Count Downs in sizes 11 and 14 have a perfect swimming action at paddling speeds.

Picking a favorite fish is difficult for Jim although yellowtail and calico bass are at the top of the list. But, he says nothing matches the thrill of a large thresher grey hounding across the surface and pulling your kayak at ten miles per hour. His largest weighed in at 172 lbs. 4 ozs., and the fight lasted two and a half hours. Still, the most exciting fish for Jim is a 180 lb. striped marlin that he hooked off the coast of La Jolla. He was using 20 lb. test line, and the big fish jumped more times than Jim can tell you. He had the fish up to the kayak twice but decided to play it safe and released it. That fight also lasted two and a half hours. If you would like to read about Jim's adventures with the striped marlin or the thresher sharks in greater detail, Ed Zieralski of the San Diego *Union Tribune* has written a series of articles about kayakfishing with Jim Sammons. Jim also has the articles posted on his website for his kayakfishing business which is known as La Jolla Kayak Fishing.

Jim has some experienced advice for new kayakfishermen. If possible, go out with an experienced guide first. It will cut years off the learning curve. If a guide isn't possible, just take it slow. Don't take out three of your best outfits on your first outings, unless you want to buy some new gear. Until you get some time under your belt, take out just one rod and go after smaller fish until you know how to handle your kayak and your epquipment. Jim says there are more than a few rods sitting at the bottom of the sea: left by inexperienced kayak fisherman off the California coast. Always err on the side of safety. Always check the weather before going out. Never paddle out farther than you can paddle back in bad weather. Carry plenty of safety equipment, including a compass, GPS, cell phone, radio, an extra paddle, a PFD, throw rope, and a first aid kit in a small dry bag. You can never be too safe.

Ken Sigvardson

Ken Sigvardson has been kayakfishing since 1996. He is a director of a pharmaceutical company, but if you spend some time talking with him, you will think that he is a guide. He is that knowledgeable and experienced. Ken is from Delaware, but he grew up and still fishes the northeast coast from New Jersey, to Montauk Point, and especially around Cape Cod and Martha's Vineyard. Although he fishes the Chesapeake Bay near his new home, he is more than willing to drive 8 hours to fish the northeast coast. The reason is the remoteness of many of the surf fishing areas. It is a long trip by boat to some of them, and beach access requires a four wheel drive to get to the more remote sections. The result is less fishing pressure. Striped bass are the prize, but bluefish and false albacore are a bonus.

Ken got into kayakfishing for very practical reasons. Like many surf fishermen, he was often frustrated while watching fish breaking on bait just beyond his casting range. There were usually plenty of fish about a half mile out. Sitting in his truck, he would hopelessly watch them with binoculars. Ken had heard a story from friends about a guy in a kayak spotted walloping stripers up against some rocks near shore at Squibnocket. He had seen kayakers paddling around the waters of Marthas Vineyard. He thought to himself that he could launch one of those kayaks from the surf and reach some of the visible fish out of casting range, and he could also use the kayak to find fish when they are not showing. On a return trip for a family vacation to Cape Cod, he decided to rent a kayak to give it a try. He rented a two person kayak, but during the test paddle, he learned that he should buy a one person kayak for better paddling characteristics.

Ken Sigvardson in his *Pachena* with a nice striped bass

Ken bought an *Acadia* by Perception kayaks. The *Acadia* is a single person, 12.5 ft., 50 lb., sit-on-bottom model. He instantly confirmed his thoughts that he could find big fish off the beaches where he surf fished. In fact, Ken's best kayak catch is a 48 inch, 40 lb. striped bass. He also learned that he could locate fish by trolling, especially false albacore that weigh in the teens by trolling a four inch Fin-S Fish on a light jig head behind his kayak.

Trolling is also helpful to efficiently use the time spent paddling to and from his fishing areas.

Ken later tried those rocks at Squibnocket where he had first heard of the kayaker nailing stripers. Sure enough, he hung onto a 30 lb.'er that gave him a ride along the rocks that made him appreciate the rudder installed on his new *Pachena* kayak. The rudder and strategic rod positioning helped to keep his newer, more expensive kayak hull a little further out from the rocks than the striper had in mind. Ken had a little trouble stuffing the big fish into the front cargo hatch. He had to bend the tail.

Now Ken doesn't go surf fishing without a couple of kayaks strapped to the roof of his 4WD. He needs an extra kayak now because his 19 year old son Derek is also a kayakfishing fanatic. Derek has caught one of those finicky but hard fighting false albacore weighing in at 12 lbs. Kayakfishing fever is spreading. One of Ken's best fishing buddies has also purchased a kayak.

Ken's favorite kayak is the *Pachena* by Current Designs, but he usually recommends the *Acadia* by Perception Kayaks to beginners because it is cheaper (under $500), wider and more initially stabile. It is also easier for beginners to paddle. The *Pachena*, though it costs more, has a deeper cockpit and better handling characteristics. It is not as wide as the *Acadia,* so it paddles more efficiently, but it begins to lean more easily when you shift your weight. However, after the initial leaning, it stabilizes which leads to the term *secondary stability*. For such superior design characteristics, you will pay more than three times as much for the *Pachena* at about $1800. Small differences can make all the difference to a kayak fisherman. The deeper cockpit of the *Pachena* allows Ken to place an Igloo Playmate cooler inside the cockpit. The cooler, which has a volume capable of carrying a six pack of drinks, is used instead to carry live eels which are his ammunition of choice for large striped bass on the northeast coast.

Ken offers a few words for kayak anglers that want to tangle with the bigger fish. He says that the complications of dealing with a large fish and the kayak at the same time take some getting used to. But don't worry, because eventually it all becomes second nature and very exciting. He recommends securing a pair of pliers and a small hand gaff to the deck where you can access them easily when handling a big fish. Ken wrote an excellent and informative article on kayakfishing the northeast coast which can be found on the Internet at the Stripersurf.com website. You can contact Ken by email at sigvark@attglobal.net.

Capt. Allen Cartmell

Capt. Allen Cartmell is a kayakfishing guide working out of Port Oconnor, Texas. He has to drive 30 miles to the nearest grocery store, but he's surrounded by redfish and seatrout. He just has to go out to get the breadcrumbs. Allen has been kayaking since 1995 and kayakfishing since 1996, but he grew up fishing in the waters around Galveston with his father who was also a fishing guide. A friend turned him on to kayakfishing, and he says it was instant love. Now he spends his days guiding kayakfishermen on Shoalwater Bay, Mule Slough and Contee Lake areas of Port Oconner. Allen and his clients fly out over the thin waters on his shallow running tunnel drive flatsboat which is also equipped with four Aquaterra *Prisms*. The *Prisms* are customized for fishing with rodholders, extra storage hatches, soft coolers for drinks, floating stringers and a net. Allen was recently featured in the November-December 1999 issue of the prestigious *Tide Magazine*. The magazine is the official publication of the Coastal Conservation Association which is the watchguard of our coastal gamefish populations.

Al has a unique solution for keeping a kayak stationary while casting to a position or while fighting a fish. He uses a long wooden dowel with a sharpened end pushed down through a scupper hole to stake out the kayak in the bottom sand or muck. This technique would also work well as a solution for fishing along mangroves where large snook or redfish often pull the kayak in toward the mangroves and cut off the line on the oyster shells encrusted on the root systems.

Allen likes to use light tackle. He and his clients seldom use live bait. Instead, they throw topwater plugs, spoons, and soft plastic baits. When flyrodding, the popular spoonflies get the action. He specializes in redfish and seatrout which often results in his clients catching their limits. His clients span a wide range of age and physical ability. He's guided kayakfishermen up to 70 years of age. Al's goal for his kayakfishing is to keep anglers paddling. He has some advice for beginners. Relax, anybody can do it.

Jackson Reade

Jackson Reade, is a computer consultant and kayakfishing guide. He longed for the old days when fishing on Florida's saltwater flats was not so crowded, especially with so many high powered flatsboats that suddenly appeared along the Banana and Indian Rivers where he loves to fish. So Jackson packed up his fishing gear and a canoe and headed for the *no motor zone* of the Banana River, also known as the *NMZ*. There he could pursue redfish, snook, seatrout, black drum and tarpon in an environment where they behave normally without the constant roar of outboard motors causing them to flee the shallow waters where they like to feed. He used the canoes for awhile, but he wanted something faster, stealthier and more maneuverable.

Then he tried a kayak. That was 1995, and he has never looked back. No wonder. From the kayak, he has caught redfish over 50 inches some of which probably weighed close to 40 lbs. Jackson's favorite fish though is the snook because of how much more aggressively they strike than the other fish on the flats. Because of their speed, he compares them to oversized bonefish that can jump. He believes the snook is also one of the most beautiful fish on the flats.

Jackson likes to use light spinning rods from his kayak. He uses 10 lb. Berkley Fireline with a low visibility 20 lb. flourocarbon leader. He uses the kayak to position himself upwind or downwind from a school of fish such as redfish. If the fish are very spooky from fishing pressure, he notes their direction of travel and paddles well ahead of them and lays out some baits to fish very slowly in the path of their approach. He will use artificial, live, or cut baits.

His favorite artificial baits are jerkbaits, especially Shad Assassins and Zoom Salty Superflukes. If he was limited to taking one lure, it would be a jerkbait because of its weedless characteristics and its versatility. He fishes them on top like a topwater plug, mid depths like a lipped diving plug, and on bottom like a grub or Texas rigged worm. If the fish are too spooky for artificials, he usually has a few ladyfish onboard that they catch and cut up for redfish which seem to favor them over other cut baits. The reds do not seem to care if it is alive or dead. For live baits, he favors live finger mullet for big trout and tarpon. Jackson has a neat setup for his livebait. He has a 5 gallon bucket in a hatch behind his seat in his Aquaterra *Prism* kayaks. The hatch has a cutout that is custom fitted to receive the bucket. He uses an airstone aerator from Marine Metal Products called Big Bubbles. The aerator runs on lightweight and convenient D cell flashlight batteries.

The *Shearwater KV* from Heritage Kayaks is his favorite kayak. The reason is speed and distance. The NMZ is a big body of water and Jackson wants to know *what's going on* everywhere. When not with clients, he can really cover some water in this kayak. When he is with clients, he can do some high speed scouting around while they are busy fishing. It is an expensive kayak because it is not rotomolded. It is manufactured from composite materials including hand laid fibreglass, carbon and kevlar. It is a big kayak at 18 ft. 3 inches, and it has won some prestigous races. It may be the fastest kayak on the water. Go Jackson! At 24 inches wide, it has moderate stability. In waist deep water, it is stabile enough to climb in and out of without tipping over.

Jackson is big on wading. In fact, he says that he spends 50 per cent of his fishing time wading. He feels that wading is even stealthier than fishing from the kayak, and the extra height of a standing angler is an advantage over a seated angler while sightfishing. In addition, wading allows an angler to cover an area more thoroughly. He feels that fishermen who avoid wading are missing out on a lot of fish. He also kayakfishes and wades the backcountry skinny waters of Mosquito Lagoon where the big boats cannot penetrate, the north end of the Indian River, and the South Banana River. Jackson's advice to new kayakfishermen is to get a kayak that is right for the type of kayakfishing that you are going to use it for. If you have to cover distances, get a boat that is long enough, tracks well, and has some speed. If you are going to fish open water, get a seaworthy kayak with a rudder. If you do not need the distance and will be fishing closed water, get a shorter, wider and more stabile kayak. Jackson feels that kayakers often do not give enough consideration to their paddle selection. Getting an expensive kayak and a cheap paddle is like buying a Corvette with a four cylinder engine.

Jackson Reade's kayakfishing goal is to achieve a grand slam of a redfish, a seatrout, a snook and a tarpon in one day by either himself or a client. He has come close several times. If you are connected to the Internet, a visit to his website is really worth the trip. It's a virtual adventure almost as good as taking the actual trip there.

Capt. Butch Rickey

My first kayaking experience almost turned me off to the sport because I was soaked to my waist sitting in 6 inches of water all day. They had me in the wrong kayak!

Florida flatsfishing guide, Capt. Butch Rickey, is a big guy. Butch was looking for an alternative to flatsboats and an alternative way to stalk tailing redfish on his home waters from Sarasota Bay to Pine Island Sound on the Gulf coast of Florida. Fortunately, they found him the right kayak since he has now been kayakfishing since 1997. He now uses the Perception *Swing* which is great for larger anglers, and it is stable and reasonably dry. It is also easily rigged for fishing, and Butch has added rodholders fore and aft. He also installed a rudder and a high back seat. Butch's kayak purchasing advice is to *try before you buy*, and make sure it is for you.

Redfish are Butch's personal favorite, but he also fishes for snook, seatrout, jack crevalle, ladyfish, tripletail, and gag grouper. Some of Butch's more notable catches have been made with live bait, including some outstanding catches of 50-70 snook and redfish in one day. Capt. Butch prefers live bait for putting customers on fish, but he personally likes fishing artificials, and he says that you just cannot beat a 1/2 oz. Johnson Silver Minnow in gold or silver.

Butch's home range is some of the best flatsfishing that the state of Florida has to offer. You can learn a lot about fishing the Pine Island Sound area by visiting Butch's website where you will find many informative feature articles by Capt. Butch. You can also sign up to receive regular fishing reports by email. You can even register for a guided trip online. Butch runs an unusual guide service in that he will rent you kayaks to fish on your own, or he will give you the full guided tour. He will even use his flatsboat to run you and your kayak to those faraway fishing sites that are always sweeter without the hard work of the long paddle. Butch is now hooked on kayakfishing, and his goal is to introduce as many anglers as possible to the sport and to have it replace some of the power boat trips he now runs.

John Stanton

John Stanton, is a kayakfishing guide from Ft. Pierce, Florida. He is very practical rather than a romantic when it comes to kayakfishing. He says that you do not have to be a big fan of kayaking to love and appreciate the benefits of fishing from kayaks. The kayak is just a vehicle to fish from, and it is the best that he has found. John has been kayakfishing since 1991. He bought a kayak for his wife. Ongoing and frequent engine problems with his fishing boat forced John to begin fishing from the kayak when his skiff was in the repair shop. He fell in love with kayakfishing and began taking the kayak along in the skiff with him when he went fishing.

Since 1996, he has been running Alternative Fishing Charters which is a kayakfishing guide service that specializes in sightfishing for tailing fish such as redfish and bonefish. Together with his new partner, Evan Kolb, they guide kayakfishermen on the Indian River along Florida's east coast and at Islamorada in the Florida Keys. His favorite area is Mosquito Lagoon near Oak Hill because it is such a gorgeous area with top notch fishing.

John is also very practical in his kayak choice. He recently switched to the new *Tribalance* kayaks which have outriggers that allow you to stand up. As a sight fisherman, John does not have to give up the height advantage that other kayakers forsake in order to gain the kayak advantages. Not only can you stand up, but there are also two sitting positions which reduce back strain tremendously. The kayaks are faster than any sit-on-top or cockpit boat he has paddled, including his wooden 13 footer that weighs in at 36 pounds.

John is a fan of lightweight aluminum rodholders that rotate 360 degrees which are available in most kayak shops. Another neat addition to John's kayaks are a set of walkie talkies. When in groups of three or more kayaks, the walkie talkies allow the anglers to spread out, giving everyone enough space for stalking tailers, but everyone can still keep in communication with the others. John's most useful customizing addition to his kayaks is the economical and unique anchoring system. John goes to Home Depot and buys a 36 inch by 3/8 inch aluminum rod. He files one end down to a blunt point. On the other end, he drills a 1/8 inch hole. Next, he puts a stainless steel ring through the hole. To the ring, he ties a four foot piece of anchor line. On the opposite end of the line he ties a brass clip. The clip attaches to the kayak or his belt loop. The filed end of the rod is inserted into the river bottom, and John can then position it to face any direction that he needs to make a cast. Of course, it only works in shallow water, but then, that's where the tailers are to be found. Live bait normally is not used unless requested by the client, and then shrimp gets the nod. When fishing for bonefish at Islamorada, John and Evan will use crabs. Both baits survive very well in the most basic of commercial bait buckets, so there is no need for a live bait tank.

Ten pound line spinning outfits and eight weight flyrod systems with floating, weight forward flylines are the preferred weapons to hurl the lures and flies at visible targets on the skinny water flats. Capt. Mike Hakala's Flats Candy lures are used on redfish around the Titusville area, but the reds around inlets seem to prefer topwater Mirrolures such as the 7M-21. Alternative Fishing Charters caters to flyfishermen, and they recommend the Copper Liz and Redfish Candy as flies of choice for redfish.

John advises that new kayakfishermen who are former skiff fishermen should learn to use more patience to work a flat. He says that kayakfishing on the flats comes quicker to wading fishermen. He further advises anglers to make shorter casts, especially as you will be surprised at how close you can get to a fish by kayak before it spooks, but a good presentation of a fly or lure is critical. Learn to read the water surface as your ability to look into the water is reduced if you're sitting down. The ability to tell the difference between a mullet or redfish headwake is very important. On the other hand, no one is more adept at seeing a tail above the surface than someone who is practically sitting on the surface.

One of John's personal kayakfishing goals is to fish the Great Bahama Bank. He wants to be dropped off at the southern end of Andros Island and to fish his way through the flats and keys for one week. On the business side of kayakfishing, he wants to begin offering three day trips to the Dry Tortugas next year.

Rick Roberts

Rick Roberts from Sanford, Florida knows a lot about kayaks and kayakfishing. He first started kayaking in the late 1980's, and he started kayakfishing in 1992. He was the southeastern sales representative for Heritage Kayaks, and he was formerly a sales representative for Kiwi Kayaks. Rick also represents some selected accessory products related to kayaking and kayakfishing. Rick also sets up group kayaking trips and guides kayakfishermen.

Rick began his kayakfishing career while he was a representative for Kiwi Kayaks. He had sold some kayaks to a marina on the Wekiva River. He wanted to try catching some fish from his kayak while he was at the river and decided to give it a try. The water was up in the springs so the backcountry was full of fish, and Rick was able to get off the beaten track with the kayak. The kayak was able to slip over logs, thick floating vegetation and other obstructions that his canoe was not able to cross, and the kayak was more maneuverable and faster than his canoe.

Now, Rick is a major proponent and guru of kayakfishing. He is also very knowledgeable about kayak design and its application in fishing scenarios. Rick can give you a quick education on foot pounds of energy expension in various kayaks and the design characteristics that yield paddling efficiency and secondary stability. Or, he can just tell you which kayak to buy for your particular fishing situation. He'll tell you that a kayak that is best for a freshwater fishing situation and the best kayak for saltwater flatsfishing may not be the same kayak.

No matter what type of fishing he is doing, he prefers a kayak that is stable, dry and easy to paddle for a long time. Rick's favorite hull design for fishing is the Heritage Kayak design. It has a dry seat, narrow, easy-to-paddle hull and a wide hard chine sponson for added stability. It is no problem to quickly exit or enter one in either deep or shallow water. His favorite boat for small freshwater rivers and lakes is the *Osprey*. It is 13 feet, easy to paddle, reasonably dry and has lots of deck room for his small plastic tackle box and two rods. For flats fishing, he prefers the *Expedition LP*. Rick says it is the best all day fishing kayak that he is aware of for saltwater flats or big lakes because it doesn't require too much energy to paddle it for a long time.

Rick especially likes to guide for largemouth bass because he has some very special honey holes with large bass in clear shallow water. Due to the clear and shallow conditions, he prefers light tackle spinning rods with eight pound test line to make long casts. Rick also has a very special lure to catch them on. The nature of the lure must be kept top secret at this time. However, Rick does often say that in a perfect world topwater would always be the right bait. Rick also fishes for tarpon, permit, bonefish, weakfish, redfish and snook. His favorite are snook in the mangroves of the Everglades or permit on the flats of Biscayne Bay. Rick likes to wade with the kayak tethered to his belt.

Rick has two goals in kayakfishing. He has already begun

working on the first goal with the help of a couple of other fishing guides. He is designing the ultimate fishing kayak. The new kayak will be called the *Flats Stalker*, and it will be a modified version of a Heritage Kayak hull. It will have all the customized features to keep a kayakfisherman comfortable and efficient on the water in a ready to fish package. Rick's other goal is to develop a kayakfishing school. He encourages new kayakfishermen to take lessons, but cautions them to make sure the instructor is a kayakfisherman so that he will be aware of the problems you must overcome while paddling and fishing.

Jeff Krieger

Kayakfishing guide Jeff *Rhino* Krieger already has many years of experience at fishing from kayaks. He has been guiding since 1990. Born in Oahu, Hawaii and raised in Santa Barbara, California, he was not allowed to use the family's Boston Whaler at a tender age. So, he started fishing early from kayaks. (Many of us are finishing up in our kayaks, having sold our Boston Whalers and bassboats.) Jeff learned mostly by trial and error in those early years, but he also got a lot of help from Dad, Grandpop and his uncles. In addition to California waters, Jeff has fished the waters of Mexico and Hawaii, and he has hopes to fish Alaska and the Midway Islands.

Jeff regularly catches calico bass, sand bass, rockfish and assorted less desirable members of the ecosystem. His most notable catch is a 50 lb. California halibut. He has also caught a very impressive 52 lb. white seabass, but he rates his *wall-to-wall halibut* as his best catch because it was closest to the state record and because he had been trying to nail one of that size for a long time. Jeff has also landed big thresher sharks—which California kayakfishermen are famous for— up to 170 lbs. He has set his big fish goals on a marlin and a tuna over 100 lbs. Jeff likes fishing for the white seabass and the halibut most because they are great fights and great eating. He is generally a catch and release fisherman, but every now and then he has a taste for *BBQ*. Some of Jeff's meals get a little large and need to be tied up with

with a rope and towed back to shore. More about that later.

Jeff likes to use a combination of live and artificial baits. He carries a rod rigged for catching bait and a trolling bucket to keep about a dozen alive. He also uses a wide variety of artificial lures including plastic swimming baits, spoons and jigs. If his fishfinder is showing good numbers of fish under the kayak, he will fish the entire water column, but if he is targetting halibut, he keeps his jig bouncing along the bottom. The 50 lb. halibut hit a white bucktail jig, and the 52 lb. white seabass hit a white plastic swimming bait. His favorite tackle for fishing his baits is a Shimano 400s reel with 15 lb. test clear mono and a medium/heavy rod of at least 7 feet in length with good power for lifting heavy fish up to his kayak.

Once up at the kayak, Jeff ties the bigger fish off with a rope to his RHYNOBAR which is a fish handling aid that Jeff designed and markets to other kayakfishermen. The RHYNOBAR is a stainless steel bar that spans the width of the kayak on the forward deck. Solidly connected to the kayak, it is a sturdy place to tie off a large fish while towing it in toward shore. It also serves as a secure attachment site for depthfinders and rodholders. Jeff uses Scotty's rail mounted rodholders with leashes attached to the RHYNOBAR. In addition to his depthfinder, which also attaches to the RHYNOBAR, Jeff equips his Ocean Kayak *Malibu Two* with drift chutes (sea anchors), gaff, net, dry bags, small cooler, cut-away-knife, handheld VHF radio, and a compass. The *Malibu Two* is Jeff's favorite kayak right now because it is big enough for him and all his gear plus a 150 lb. thresher shark if he needs to transport a client's catch. Jeff advises new kayak anglers to start simple, adding epquipment as they grow into their kayak. He says to find a kayak that fits you and your style of fishing.

Dennis Spike

No list of kayakfishermen, no matter how long or short, can be completed without the addition of Dennis Spike. Dennis owns and operates Coastal Kayak Fishing in Reseda, California. More importantly, he owns the Coastal Kayak Fishing Website on the Internet which has had such a tremendous influence to promote kayakfishing. In particular, his bulletin board service is a clearing house where both experienced and neophyte kayakfishermen exchange ideas. Coastal Kayak Fishing offers guided kayakfishing trips, kayakfishing instruction, and kayakfishing accessories. They also distribute kayakfishing educational materials and news on and off the Internet. Dennis distributes his *Yak Attack* newsletter in hardcopy which is the only periodical devoted strictly to kayakfishing.

Dennis has been kayakfishing since the mid 80's. He and his cousin purchased kayaks on a hunch that they might be useful to fish from off the California coast after his cousin moved closer to the beach. Dennis says the decision was born out of pure fishing passion. He says that he is still searching for his favorite fishing kayak. He only considers about ten sit-on-top models on the market to be truly fishable. For offshore big game fishing, he prefers a fairly wide, medium size, sit-on-bottom style kayak. On buying a kayak, he advises to *try before you buy*. Dennis has fished most of the North American fisheries by kayak, and all of the big tunas are his favorite species. His favorite lure on his home waters of southern California and the Baja peninsula is a chrome spoon, and it would also be his choice if he could choose only one lure. For live bait, his best choice is a 4 inch mackeral.

Dennis believes that the sport of kayakfishing is here to stay. He says it is a trend and not a fad, and that the sport lends a unique perspective to those who participate. Since the number of people who will participate is small, we will be able to share our waterways without crowding and to fish areas otherwise off limits or inaccessible to others. The passion in each kayakfisherman is common to all, and most kayakfishermen are committed to the sport for life. He states that kayakfishing is the greatest sport ever conceived. It allows people to experience fishing in a way that was, until recently, only achievable with great expenditure of money and non fishing time. The attention paid to coastal clean ups and fishery management has benefited the fisheries significantly over the past two decades, awakening ecosystems that were suffering greatly. As kayakfishermen, we need strong voices to impact the good of the fisheries. Dennis wants to kayakfish the world and use his good fortune to effect a positive impact on the fisheries for generations to come.

Chapter Seventeen

Kayakfishing Resources

Kayak Companies

Cobra Kayaks
(310) 327-9216
cobrakayaks@worldnet.att.net
www.cobrakayaks.com

Current Designs
770 Enterprise Crescent,
Victoria, B.C. V8Z 6R4
(507) 454-5430
info@cdkayak.com
www.cdkayak.com

Heritage kayaks
55 Ballou Blvd.
Bristol, RI 02809
(401) 253-0401
www.heritagekayaks.com

Hobie Cat Company
4925 Oceanside Blvd.
Oceanside CA 92056
(760) 758-9100
USAHobie@aol.com
www.hobiecat.com

Kiwi Kayak Co., Inc.
2454 Vista Del Monte
Concord, CA 94520
(800) K-4-KAYAK
mail@kiwikayak.com
www.kiwikayak.com

Necky Kayaks
1100 Riverside Road
Abbotsford, BC V2S 7P1
(604) 850-1206
www.necky.com/

Ocean Kayak
2460 Salashan Loop
PO Box 5003
Ferndale, WA 98248
(800) 8-KAYAKS

www.oceankayak.com/

Necky Kayaks
1100 Riverside Road
Abbotsford, BC
V2S 7P1
(604) 850-1206
www.necky.com/

Paluski Boats Limited
c/o Adventure Fitness
County Rd 18 at Hwy 507
RR #3, Lakefield, Ontario KOL 2HO
(705) 652-7986
paluski@oncomdis.on.ca
www.kawartha.com/boats

Perception, Inc.
111 Kayaker Way
P.O Box 8002
Easley, SC 29641-8002
(864) 859-7518
mktg@kayaker.com
www.kayaker.com

Tribal Kayaks
930 Apple Blossom Drive
Villa Hills, Ky 41017
(800)587-4225
www.tribalance.com

Wilderness Systems
PO Box 4339
Archdale, NC 27263
(800) 311-7245
cservice@wildsys.com
www.wildsys.com

Kayaking Books

Kayaking: A Beginner's Manual
by Nigel Foster
Fenhurst Books; ISBN: 1898660522

Sit-On-Top Kayaking: A Beginner's Guide

by Tom Holtey
GeoOdyssey Publications;
ISBN: 0966865502

Kayaking Magazines

Canoe & Kayak Magazine
PO Box 3146, 10526 NE 68th St.
Kirkland, WA 98083
www.canoekayak.com/

Kanawa
Box 398 Merrickville,
Ontario, Canada KOG 1NO
(888) 252-6292
www.crca.ca

Paddler
PO Box 775450
Steamboat Springs, CO 80477
(888) 774-7554
www.paddlermagazine.com

Kayaking Magazines Online

Atlantic Coastal Kayaker
www.qed.com/ack
* starting to post kayakfishing articles

Kanawa
www.crca.ca

Paddler
www.paddlermagazine.com

Sea Kayaker Magazines
www.seakayaker.com

Kayakfishing Accessories

Anchors

Action Watersports
402 Progress Rd.
Auburndale, FL 33823
(941) 967-4148
Email: dsims1@gte.net
www.actionwatersports.net

Coastal Kayakfishing
6753 Tampa Avenue
Reseda, CA. 91335

(818) 345-5824
www.kayakfishing.com

West Marine Inc
500 Westridge Drive
Watsonville, CA 95076-4100
(831) 728-2700

Apparel

Navarro Weather Gear
201-975 Vernon Drive
Vancouver, BC, Canada
V6A 3P2
(604) 251-1756
info@navarrogear.com
www.navarrogear.com
*Great kayaking clothing-neoprene
suits & Navskin

Planetary Gear
6350 Gunpark Drive,
 Boulder, CO. 80301
(303) 581-0518
www.planetarygear.com

RapidStyle
4300 Howard Ave.
Kensington, MD 20895
(301) 564-0459
www.rapidstyle.com

Salamander, Inc
PO Box 1363
Bend, OR 97709
(541) 388.1821
play@salamanderpaddlegear.com
www.salamanderpaddlegear.com

Backrests

Surf to Summit
132 Robin Hill Road
Santa Barbara, CA
(800) 930-8782
www.surftosummit.com/

Cartop carriers- foam

Action Watersports
402 Progress Rd.
Auburndale, FL 33823

(941) 967-4148
Email: dsims1@gte.net
www.actionwatersports.net

Coastal Kayakfishing
6753 Tampa Avenue
Reseda, CA. 91335
(818) 345-5824
www.kayakfishing.com/

Ocean Kayak
2460 Salashan Loop
PO Box 5003
Ferndale, WA 98248
(800) 8-KAYAKS
www.oceankayak.com/

Cartop carriers- standard

Sports Rack Vehicle Outfitters
2401 Arden Way
Sacramento, CA 95825
(916) 648-9200; fax (916) 648-9209
www.sportsrack.com

Yakima Products
1385 8th Street
Arcata, CA 95521
(888) 925-0703
www.yakima.com

Dry Bags

Action Watersports
402 Progress Rd.
Auburndale, FL 33823
(863) 967-4148
Email: dsims1@gte.net
www.actionwatersports.net

Coastal Kayakfishing
6753 Tampa Avenue
Reseda, CA. 91335
(818) 345-5824
http://www.kayakfishing.com/

Jacks Plastic Welding Inc
Jack Kloepfer
115 South Main
Aztec, NM 87410
(505) 334 8748
http://web.frontier.net/jacks/

repweld.html
jacks@frontier.net

Watershed
2000 Riverside Drive
Asheville, N.C. 28804
(800) 811-8607
www.drybags.com

Dry Boxes

Cases4Less.com
9640-B Mission Gorge Road #305
Santee, CA 92071
(619) 449-8044
service@cases4less.com
http://www.cases4less.com

Otter Products, LLC
316 S. Link Lane
Fort Collins, Colorado 80524
(888) 695-8820
info@otterbox.com
www.otterbox.com

Insulated Bags

Muleworks, Inc. -The Icemule Cooler
PO Box 1955
Richmond, VA 23218
sales@muleworks.com
http://store.yahoo.com/mule/

Kayak Carts

Coastal Kayakfishing
6753 Tampa Avenue
Reseda, CA. 91335
(818) 345-5824
http://www.kayakfishing.com/

Montura Sports Co.
PO Box 49852
Los Angeles, CA 90049
(310) 915-4174
Email: achaux@earthlink.com

Ocean Kayak
2460 Salashan Loop
PO Box 5003
Ferndale, WA 98248
(800) 8-KAYAKS

http://www.oceankayak.com/

Roleez Wheel Systems
Toteez II
5717 Sellger Drive
Norfolk, VA 23502
(800) 369-1390 (757) 461-1122
www.roleez.com

Livewells & Aerators

Aquatic Ecosystems
1767 Benbow Ct
Apopka, FL 32703
(407) 886-3939
Email: aes@aquaticeco.com
www.aquaticeco.com

Bass Pro Shops
2500 E. Kearney
Springfield, MO 65898-0123
(800) 227-7776
www.basspro.com

Baitsaver
Cabela's
One Cabela Drive
Sidney, Nebraska 69160
(800) 237-4444
www.cabelas.com

Keep Alive Inc
PO Box 1952
Tarpon Springs, Fl
34688
(727) 841-0407

Oxygenation Systems of Texas
PO Box 383, Kinser Rd.
Anahuac, Texas 77514
(409) 267-6458
Email: oxyedge@ih2000.net

Live Bait Supplies

Aquatic Ecosystems
1767 Benbow Ct
Apopka, FL 32703
(407) 886-3939
Email: aes@aquaticeco.com
www.aquaticeco.com

Miscellaneous

The Lipper
Wheelhouse Products
70 Moshassuck
Lincoln, RI 02865
(800) 450-2930

RHYNOBAR
c/o Jeff Krieger
6768 Sandalwood Drive
Simi Valley, CA 93063
(805) 520-9713
info@rhynobar.net
www.rhynobar.net/

Kayak Repair & Instructions

Jacks Plastic Welding Inc
Jack Kloepfer
115 South Main
Aztec, NM 87410
(505) 334 8748
http://web.frontier.net/jacks/
repweld.html
jacks@frontier.net

Rivets & Rivet Guns

Action Watersports
402 Progress Rd.
Auburndale, FL 33823
(941) 967-4148
Email: dsims1@gte.net
www.actionwatersports.net

Rodholders

Bass Pro Shops
2500 E. Kearney
Springfield, MO 65898-0123
(800) 227-7776
www.basspro.com

Coastal Kayakfishing
6753 Tampa Avenue
Reseda CA 91335
(818) 345-5824
Spike@kayakfishing.com
www.kayakfishing.com

Il Endeavors-First Mate
85 Glencrest Blvd.
Toronto, Ontario Canada M4B1L7
(416) 755-9304
Email: aboo@idirect.com
http://webhome.idirect.com/~aboo/

Trailers

Trailex Aluminum Products
PO Box 553
60 Industrial Park Drive
Canfield, OH 44406-0553
(800) 282-5042
info@trailex.com
www.trailex.com

Kayakfishing Clubs

California Club

Ventura County Kayak and Fishing Club
http://ljohnsen.digitalchainsaw.com/
KAYAK.HTM

Texas Club

P.A.C.K.
c/o Wilderness Furnishings, Inc.
5420 Manor Drive
Sugarland, Texas 77479
(281) 403-9013
wildfur@scci.com
www.wildfur.com

Kayakfishing Guides

California

Gary Bulla
1290 East Main St.
Santa Paula, Ca. 93060
(805) 933-1366
Glbulla@aol.com
www.garybulla.com

Jeff Krieger
6768 Sandalwood Drive
Simi Valley, CA 93063
(805) 520-9713
nfo@rhynobar.net
http://www.rhynobar.net

Jim Sammons
La Jolla Kayakfishing
7625 Melotte St.
San Diego, CA 92119
(619) 461-7172
http://www.kayak4fish.com
Kayak4Fish@aol.com

Dennis Spike
c/o Coastal Kayak Fishing
6753 Tampa Avenue
Reseda CA 91335
(818) 345-5824
Spike@kayakfishing.com
http://www.kayakfishing.com

Florida

Capt. Ken Daubert
Florida Kayak Fishing
3323 SE 2nd Street
Ocala, FL 34471
(352) 624-1878
CptKen2@floridakayakfishing.com

Jackson Read
(407) 421-1042
flatyakers@yahoo.com
http://flatskayakfishing.com

Capt. Butch Rickey
1610 Palmetto Ave.
Lehigh Acres, FL 33936
(800) 545-1853
http://www.barhoppr.com/kayaks.htm
capt@barhoppr.com

Rick Roberts
Florida Outback
261 Nova Dr.
Sanford, Fl 32771
(407) 302-5550
Webpaddler@intersrv.com

John Stanton
Alternative Fishing Charters
911 Emerald Ave.
Ft. Pierce, FL 34945
(561) 468-0209
Fishkayaks@aol.com

Ultimate Kayak Fishing
Montauk Long Island, NY
& Key West Bight Marina, Key West
Florida
(877) 529-2534
email: info@ultimatekayakfishing.com

New York

Ultimate Kayak Fishing
Montauk Long Island, NY
& Key West Bight Marina, Key West
Florida
(877) 529-2534
email: info@ultimatekayakfishing.com

Texas

Capt. Alan Cartmell
PO Box 335
Port O'Connor, TX 77982-0335
(361) 983-2746
Email: shanut83@aol.com

Barry P. Evans
3804 Quail Run
Granbury, TX 76049
(817) 326-3572

Kayakfishing Tours

Baja Outdoor Activities
P.O. Box 792
Col.Centro
La Paz, BCS, CP 23000
MEXICO
Tel: +52-112-556-36
www.kayactivities.com/
boa@kayactivities.com

Gary Bulla
1290 East Main St.
Santa Paula, Ca. 93060
(805) 933-1366
Glbulla@aol.com
www.garybulla.com

Coastal Kayakfishing
6753 Tampa Avenue
Reseda, CA. 91335
(818) 345-5824
www.kayakfishing.com/

Kayakfishing Websites

Business sites:

Action Watersports
http://www.actionwatersports.net

Coastal Kayakfishing Website
http://www.kayakfishing.com

Florida Kayak Fishing
http://www.floridakayakfishing.com

Gary Bulla's Fly Fishing Adventures
http://www.garybulla.com

Il Endeavors-First Mate
http://webhome.idirect.com/~aboo/

La Jolla Kayakfishing
http://www.kayak4fish.com

Kayak Corner
www.socalkayakfishing.com

RHYNOBAR
http://www.rhynobar.net/

Ultimate Directory Of Kayaking Links
http://home.adelphia.net/~kwinter/
kayakmain.html

Ultimate Kayak Fishing
http://www.ultimatekayakfishing.com

Root Beer Barrell Surf and Kayak
http://www.rbbsurf.com/

Personal sites:

Extreme Kayak Fishing
http://www.kayakfish.com

Kayakfishing in Florida
http://web.tampabay.rr.com/sshell1/
kayakfishing_in_florida.htm

Kayak Fishing Texas
http://www.geocities.com/rwzewe/

Kayak Korner
http://www.socalkayakfishing.com

Ultimate Directory Of Kayaking Links
http://home.adelphia.net/~kwinter/kayakmain.html

Yakfishing.com
http://www.yakfishing.com/

Maps

Mapblast
http://www.mapblast.com

Mapquest
http://www.mapquest.com

Microsoft Terraserver Website
http://terraserver.microsoft.com

Tides

Tide Prediction Site (Unniversity of South Carolina)
http://tbone.biol.sc.edu/tide/sitesel.html

Weather Service

National Weather Service, NOAA
1325 East-West Highway
Silver Spring, MD 20910
http://www.nws.noaa.gov/

Weather Underground
http://www.wunderground.com
* great satellite photos of cloud cover

The Weather Channel
http://www.weather.com
* good radar map

Weather Radio

Speedtech Instruments
(800) 760-0004
info@speedtech.com
http://www.speedtech.com

Paddleshops

Kayakfishing Spoken Here:

California

Carlsbad Paddlesports
2780 Carlsbad Blvd, Carlsbad, Ca 92008
Phone/Fax: (760) 434-8686
kayak@inetaccess.com

Channel Islands Kayak Center
3600 S. Harbor Blvd. Suite 213
Oxnard, CA 93035
(805) 984-5995
sales@cikayak.com
http://www.cikayak.com/

Paddle Sports of Santa Barbara
100 State Street
Santa Barbara, CA 93101
(805) 568-0583

Cayucos Outfitters
136 Ocean Front
Cayucos, CA 93430
(805) 995-1993
info@gcfsurf.com
http://www.gcfsurf.com
* Offer kayakfishing trips

Maryland

Island Creek Outfitters
PO Box 93
9250 Broomes Island Rd
Broomes Island, Maryland 20615
(410) 286-0950
islcrkoutfitters@chesapeake.net
http://www.icout.com

New Jersey

Root Beer Barrell Surf and Kayak
301 10th Street South,
Brigantine, NJ 08203
(609) 266-2505
rbbsurf@dandy.net
http://www.rbbsurf.com/

Florida

Action Watersports
402 Progress Rd.
Auburndale, FL 33823
(863) 967-4148
http://www.actionwatersports.net

Estero River Outfitters
20991 S Tamiami Trail
Estero, FL 33928
(941) 992-4050
http://www.all-florida.com/
swestero.htm

The Canoe Shop
1129 Beck Avenue
Panama City, FL 32401
(850) 763-2311
http://www.paddlenorthflorida.com
*publish articles on how to get started
kayakfishing at their website

The Canoe Shop
1115B W. Orange
Tallahassee, FL 32310
(904) 576-5335
http://www.paddlenorthflorida.com
*publish articles on how to get started
kayakfishing at their website

Osprey Bay Kayaks
17952 US Hwy 19 N.
Clearwater, Fl. 33764
(727)-524-9670
Toll Free: 877-kayaks2
kayak@ospreybay.com
http://www.ospreybay.com/
*have a kayakfishing discussion group
on their website

Wade Clark Auctions
314 Reid Ave.
Port Saint Joe, FL 32456
(850) 229-9282
wcauctions@digitalexp.com
* husband and wife are avid new
kayakfishermen

Texas

Canoesport
5808 South Rice Ave.
Houston, Texas 77081
(713) 660-7000
info@canoesport.com
http://www.canoesport.com/
* have their own kayak hull which they
customize for fishing- The Ultimate Fishing Machine - ask for Charles Duvic

Southwest Paddlesports
26322 I-45 N
Spring, Texas 77386
(800) 937-2335
email: info@paddlesports.com
http://www.paddlesports.com
* home to a bunch of kayakers who also
love to fish

Wilderness Furnishings, Inc.
5420 Manor Drive
Sugarland, Texas 77479
(281) 403-9013
wildfur@scci.com
http://www.wildfur.com
*sponsors a kayakfishing club

Virginia

Shenandoah River Outfitters
Luray, VA 22835
(800) 6 CANOE 2
http://www.shenandoah-river.com

Index

Index

Invitation:

To join the Kayakfishing Revolution and the Kayakfishing Community. Become a part of the "next edition". Be a part of the on-going development of this sport.

If you are a marine dealer, paddleshop, or tackleshop with an interest in helping others to get started in kayakfishing or if you have a product of special interest to kayakfishermen, then you may want to be included in our kayakfishing resources section of the book.

We are also interested in kayakfishermen with new kayak customizing ideas, kayakfishing techniques or unusual success with any species of fresh or saltwater fish.

And we are especially interested in new or experienced kayakfishermen who have been helped by reading this book.

Please call or write or email:

Capt. Ken Daubert
3323 S.E. 2nd Street
Ocala, FL 34471

352-624-1878

CptKen2@floridakayakfishing.com

If you would like additional information about kayakfishing, especially in the state of Florida, please visit our website at:

http://www.floridakayakfishing.com

To order a quick copy:

By telephone: (352) 624-1878 (leave a clear message on recorder)

By email: CptKen2@floridakayakfishing.com

Postal orders: Coelacanth Communications, Ken Daubert, 3323 S.E. 2nd Street, Ocala, FL 34471-2947

Name:_____

Address:_____

City:_____ **State:**_____ **Zip:**_____

Telephone:_____

Email address:_____

Please send **$15.95** per book: plus

Sales tax: Please add 6% for books shipped to Florida addresses.

Shipping:

US: Add $4 for the first book and $2 for each additional book

International: Add $9 for the 1st book and $5 for each additional book.

Payment: Check_____ Credit card_____

Visa_____ Mastercard_____ Discover_____

Card number:_____

Name on card:_____**Exp. date:**_____

If you are a book distributor, catalogue, website, paddleshop, tackle shop, or an organization interested in purchasing multiple copies, please contact us for discount terms at the above listed address, phone, or email address.

Coming in 2001

How to make your

Fishing Lure Fortune

Starting with nothing

Written by 19 year professional fishing guide Capt. Ken Daubert

Designer of the famous, patented Banjo Minnow weedless fishing lure featured on TV that did 26 million dollars in sales in it's first year and eventually became a 40 million dollar winner.

Founding member and former vice president of Banjo Buddies Inc.

From digging the hole in his back yard to build a 14,000 gallon fish tank to producing an international award winning infomercial, Ken lived out his life long dream to invent a fishing lure and

retire rich

Learn:

How to promote, market & sell your fishing lure or product and

How to find talented, experienced partners

How to make and structure deals

How to protect your product from unscrupulous contacts

How to get patents, partners, manufacturing, video production, TV advertising, telemarketing, fulfillment, funding, legal services, etc.,etc.

for nothing

Also learn from the experiences of other successful entrepreneurs and how they were successful at making their fishing lure fortunes.

You also get a resources section with valuable contacts from every facet of business from designing & manufacturing to marketing & legal.